CHICAGO CHAPTER
NATIONAL SOCIETY
DAUGHTERS OF THE AMERICAN REVOLUTION

ORGANIZED MARCH 20, 1891
INCORPORATED MAY 11, 1912

Chicago Chapter NSDAR
332 South Michigan Avenue
Lower Level Suite #C356
Chicago IL, 60604

August 2019

CHICAGO CHAPTER THE FIRST CHAPTER
ORGANIZED MARCH 20, 1891 • INCORPORATED MAY 11, 1912

Effie Beulah Reeme Osborn (Mrs. Frank Stuart) Organizing Regent

CHICAGO CHAPTER REGENTS

Effie Beulah Reeme Osborn (Mrs. Frank Stuart)	1891–1892
Frances Welles Shepard (Mrs. Henry M.)	1892–1893
Ellen Rountree Jewett (Mrs. John N.)	1893–1895
Louise Dickenson Sherman (Mrs. Penoyer L.)	1895–1896
Emeline Tait Walker (Mrs. James H.)	1896–1897
Julia Booth Dickinson (Mrs. Frederick)	1897–1899
Alice Bradford Wiles (Mrs. Robert Hall)	1899–1901
Nannie McCormick Coleman (Mrs. J. A.)	1901–1903
Laura C. S. Fessenden (Mrs. B.A.)	1903–1905
Rose E. Lytton (Mrs. Henry C.)	1905–1905
Clary Cooley Becker (Mrs. Frederick W.)	1905–1906
Ida E. S. Noyes (Mrs. LaVerne)	1906–1907
Frances Sedgwick Smith (Mrs.)	1907–1908
Luelja Zearing Gross (Mrs. J. Elsworth)	1908–1909
Bertha Coombs Wean (Mrs. Frank L.)	1909–1910
Lida Eastman Torbet (Mrs. Lewis K.)	1910–1911
Jessie Lake McMullen (Mrs. Frank R.)	1911–1913
Abby Farwell Ferry (Mrs.)	1913–1914
Jean Wylie Peck Washburne (Mrs. William Dow	1914–1916
Sarah Raymond Fitz-Williams (Mrs.)	1916–1917
Louise Hammond Austin (Mrs. William Baden)	1917–1918
Laura Hayes Fuller (Mrs. Frank Revillo)	1918–1919
Cora L. Childs Greene (Mrs. T. Henry)	1919–1920
Mabel Hurd Walker Herrick (Mrs. Charles E.)	1920–1922
Luelja Zearing Gross (Mrs. J. Elsworth)	1922–1924
Sadie F. Earle (Mrs. Samuel William)	1924–1926
Blanche Brown Hopkins (Mrs. Louis Fowler)	1926–1928
Dora Moon Dixon (Mrs. Thomas John)	1928–1930
Anna Hull Stevens (Mrs. Raymond W.)	1930–1932
Mary Jane Belle Williamson (Mrs. William F.)	1932–1934
Sarah Alice Deneen Dickson (Mrs. Frederick J.)	1934–1936
Laura Henderson Jackson (Mrs. James Henry)	1936–1938
Gertrude Gilpin Richards (Mrs. J. DeForest)	1938–1940

PAST REGENTS, CONTINUED

Florence Deneen (Miss)	1940–1942
Lillian Chambers O'Neill (Mrs. Arthur J.)	1942–1944
Helen Cox Maass (Mrs. Herbert J.)	1944–1946
Margaret A. Okeson (Miss)	1946–1948
Mary A. Partenheimer (Mrs. Cyrus A.)	1948–1950
Virginia Sage Gibson (Mrs. Stanley)	1950–1952
Frances Deneen Birdsall (Mrs. Carl A.)	1952–1954
Virginia Healy Meyer (Mrs. Harold I.)	1954–1956
Elizabeth Dunn (Miss)	1956–1958
Elizabeth Hull Bell Lowry (Mrs. Howard A.	1958–1960
Pauline M. Blake (Mrs. Guy M.)	1960–1962
May Young Mullen (Mrs. Benjamin P.)	1962–1964
Jessie Spofford Tucker (Mrs. A. Judson)	1964–1966
Jennie Gaines Harris Dischinger Hopewell (Mrs. Earl F.)	1966–1969
F. Lynette Sherman (Miss)	1969–1972
Izeyl Marie French (Mrs. Adam)	1972–1974
Mildred Harrison Ostfeld (Mrs. David L.)	1974–1978
Evelyn Clark Linquist (Mrs. Douglas F.)	1978–1980
Frances Peers Bedard (Mrs. Antoine)	1980–1982
Nancy E. Postma (Miss)	1982–1986
Ruth Valerie McElroy Hunley (Mrs. Joseph V.)	1986–1988
Katherine Austin Lathrop (Ms.)	1988–1992
Patricia Logsdon Buckley* (Mrs. John L., Jr.)	1992–1996
B.A. Church* (Ms., married to Dennis J. Pabich Jr.)	1996–2000
Mary Elisabeth Livingstone Huske* (Mrs.)	2000–2001
Marion Samuelson Cramsie* (Mrs. James Francis)	2001–2004
B.A. Church* (Ms., married to Dennis J. Pabich Jr.)	2004–2008
Patricia Logsdon Buckley* (Mrs. John L., Jr.)	2008–2010
Christina Davis Bannon* (Mrs. John A.)	2010–2013
Patricia Sabo Bruce* (Mrs.)	2013–2015
Traci Lynn Martinez*	2015–2017
Nancy Marple Clarke* (Mrs. James P.)	2017–2019
Courtenay Robinson Wood*	present

*Regent living; all others are deceased

ORIGIN OF CHICAGO CHAPTER'S NAME
"I am told it was called "Chicago Chapter," simply because it was the first Chapter formed and other names had not been thought of."
--*Illinois State History of the Daughters of the American Revolution*

CHICAGO CHAPTER HISTORY
Many Sign the Constitution
Daughters Secure New Members of the Organization.
The Chicago Tribune, Saturday, March 21, 1891

"Yesterday morning what might be styled a genealogical event occurred in the organization of the Chicago Chapter of the Daughters of the American Revolution. About fifty women signed the constitution and became members of the new organization. Mrs. Frank Stewart Osborn, whose appointment as Regent for Chicago comes from Mrs. Benjamin Harrison, called the meeting to order and announced the list of officers as follows: Vice-Regent, Mrs. H.M. Shepard; Secretary, Mrs. A.T. Galt; Registrar, Mrs. A.L. Chetlain; Treasurer, Mrs. J.C. Bundy. The Board of Management is composed of the above officers and four other members—Mesdames Benjamin Fessenden, W.T. Block, Edwin Walker, and George Rozet. The Honorary Regents for Illinois are Mrs. Potter Palmer and Mrs. John A. Logan.

"Mrs. Osborn, Regent of the Chicago Chapter, in her address to the members said that while the great drama of the war ended a hundred years ago, the Revolution was still "Our Revolution", and that we should stand by the principles of our ancestors. One point should not be forgotten, and that was our mixed nationality. Side by side the men from every nation fought through the war, and side by side, we should stand today. She called attention to the movement to erect a statue to Mary Washington, and bespoke the assistance of the members.

"During the signing of the constitution, the ladies gave individual accounts of such ancestors as justified their claims to membership, and the air fairly teemed with the musty scent of old traditions. A letter written by one Samuel Lyman in 1778 to Andrew Adams, member of Congress, was read and a half incredulous smile was created by the fact that the epistle was six weeks in journeying from Connecticut to Pennsylvania. Many anecdotes of historical interest were related, and the meeting finally adjourned to reconvene next Wednesday morning at 11 a.m. in the Ways and Means Committee's room of the Columbian Exposition."

CHICAGO CHAPTER INSIGNIA

The gold or silver Chicago Chapter Insignia "CHICAGO • FIRST CHAPTER • NSDAR" with the numeral "1" and the Chicago Water Tower (as shown above) may be worn on the official NSDAR ribbon by Chicago Chapter members only. This is the only chapter pin that may be worn on-ribbon, in honor of Chicago being the first chapter of the NSDAR.

The gold or silver insignia pin is available for purchase for $40.00; if mailed, there is an additional charge for envelope and postage. Chicago Chapter members may contact the Chicago Chapter Insignia Committee Chair to purchase a Chicago Chapter Insignia.

PRESIDENT GENERAL, NSDAR

Denise Doring VanBuren
NSDAR Administration Building
1776 D Street N.W.
Washington, D.C. 20006-5303
202-628-1776

Theme: Rise and Shine For America

Symbol: Sun

Scripture: "Let your light shine before others that they may see your good deeds and glorify your father in heaven." Matthew 5:16

Mission: The Mission of the VanBuren Administration is to energize members to rise up in meaningful service to America and to shine by raising awareness of DAR's purpose, relevancy and vibrancy through robust public outreach. We will honor the spirit of our Revolutionary ancestors and educate the public about their sacrifices, and we will actively promote the rights and responsibilities of U.S. citizenship. Our administration goals include completing the final phase of restoration for DAR Constitution Hall; working to propel membership to 200,000; and ensuring financial stability and leadership training at every level.

NSDAR AND IL STATE ORGANIZATION OFFICERS
STATE REGENT, 2019–2021

Sharla Luken
2680 Orrington Ave.
Evanston, IL 60201-1770
Phone: (847) 456-3956,
sharlaluken8@gmail.com

Theme: Strength Through Service

Scripture: "We have as a sure and steadfast anchor of the soul, a hope that enters into the inner shrine behind the curtain"
Hebrew 6:19

Symbol: Anchor

Motto: Stay Positve, be considerate, perservere

Regent's Speech: "Serving Those Who Have Served Us"

Regent's Project: Honor and Respect for all Illinois Veterans Strengthening our Chapters

DISTRICT IV DIRECTOR, ILLINOIS STATE ORGANIZATION
Denise Leffler Burja
6604 Cobblestone Lane, Long Grove, IL 60047
(847) 949-7573 or (847) 951-7572
denise.burja@gmail.com

CHICAGO CHAPTER MEMBERS
SERVING ILLINOIS STATE & NATIONAL ORGANIZATIONS

Julia Riley Davila	State Page Co-Chairman
Erica Fornari	State VIS Co-Chairman
Nichole Swafford	District IV Corresponding Secretary
Ellen Peirce	National VAVS Representative
Sharon Peterson	National VAVS Deputy Representative
Peggy Becker	DAR Museum Docent

CHAPTER OFFICERS AND CONTACT INFORMATION

Regent (2019-2021)
Courtenay Wood   crwoodhnj@aol.com

First Vice Regent (2019-2021)
Julia Davila Riley   julia.riley.dar@gmail.com

Second Vice Regent (2018-2020)
Erica Fornari   efornari@gmail.com

Chaplain (2018-2020)
Sharon Zingery   szingery@gmail.com

Recording Secretary (2017-2019)
Becky Smart   becky.smart.dar@gmail.com

Corresponding Secretary (2018-2020)
Rhonda Robinett   rhondarobinett@gmail.com

Treasurer (2018-2020)
Nichole Swafford   Treasurer@darchicago.org

Registrar (2017-2019)
Lydia Roll   Registrar@darchicago.org

Librarian (2018-2020)
Debra Dudek   Debradudek@yahoo.com

Historian (2019-2021)
Emily Deitrick   epdeitr@aol.com

CHAPTER CONTACT INFORMATION

CHAPTER MAIL CORRESPONDENCE
Chicago Chapter, NSDAR
332 S. Michigan Ave.
Lower Level Suite - C#356
Chicago, IL 60604

CHAPTER EMAIL CORRESPONDENCE
thefirstchapter@darchicago.org

Chicago Chapter Website
www.darchicagochapter.org

Chicago Chapter DAR Facebook Page
www.facebook.com/ChicagoChapterDAR

Chicago Chapter Twitter
@darchicago

Chicago Chapter Blog
https://darchicago.wordpress.com

IL State Organization, Members Only
http://www.ildar.org/members/

National DAR Website
www.dar.org

NSDAR, Members Only
www.members.dar.org

CHAPTER COMMITTEE CHAIRS

Historic Preservation

National Day of Service, 10/12 (Commemorative Event)
Sharon Zingery & Misty Deckard

Community Service Awards
Peggy Bodine & Rebecca George

Education

DAR Good Citizens
Anne Brinsmade & Mary Witt

DAR Schools
Rhonda Robinett

Literacy Promotion
Anne Morrissy

Patriotism

American Indians
Sharon R. Peterson

The Flag of the United States/Honor Flight
Debbie Molina & Nichole Swafford

DAR Service for Veterans
Ellen Peirce

National Defense/ROTC Medals
Anne Brinsmade & Mary Witt

Women's Issues
Lisa Fox & Jeanneen Wilson

Standdown Coordinators
Lisa Fox & Saundra Shelley

CHAPTER COMMITTEE CHAIRS

Member Engagement

Children of the American Revolution
Julia Riley Davila

Hospitality
Rebecca George

Junior Membership
Caitlin Morris (2019-2020)

Lineage Research
Sharon Zingery

Membership
Lucy Kron

Member Course & New Horizons Course Coordinator
Lucy Kron

Social Media
Kristin Dudek

Sunshine Group
Nichole Swafford

Volunteer Genealogists
Lydia Roll

Administration

Audit Committee
Erica Fornari, Chair, Barbara Covell & Maria Stanton

Chapter History Book Sales
Peggy Becker

CHAPTER COMMITTEE CHAIRS

Chapter Master Report
Courtenay Wood

Chapter Photographers
Sharon Zingery, Misty Deckard and Rebecca George

Insignia & Chapter Pin
Pat Buckley

Parliamentarian
Alexandra Mihalas

Protocol
B. A. Church

Volunteer Information Specialists
Erica Fornari

Ways & Means
Julia Davila Riley, Chair, Courtenay Wood & Nichole Swafford

Yearbook
Rhonda Robinett

OTHER DAR COMMITTEES

These committees currently do not have a chair. They are available for a Member Course Project or New Horizons Capstone Project. Please contact Lucy Kron l_kron@msn.com if you are interested in one of these committees.

Americanism
American Heritage
American History
Commemorative Events
Community Classroom
Community Service Awards
Conservation
Constitution Week

DAR Magazine
DAR Project Patriot
DAR Scholarships
Genealogical Records
Historic Preservation
Junior American Citizens
Patriot Records Project

CHAPTER CHAIRS/LIAISON BOARD MEMBERS

While each committee chair reports directly to the Regent,
Board members act as a liaison to bring committee updates to board
meetings. Below is a list of each Board member and their liaison team.

Regent
Chapter Master Report
Audit

First Vice Regent
C.A.R.
Hospitality
Ways & Means

Second Vice Regent
Commemorative Events
VIS
Service to America

Chaplain
American Indians
Insignia
Sunshine Club

Recording Secretary
DAR Good Citizens
National Defense/ROTC Medals
The Flag of the United States
of America/Honor Flight

Corresponding Secretary
DAR Schools
PR & Media
Yearbook

Treasurer
Community Service Awards
DAR Service for Veterans

Registrar
Junior Membership
Lineage Research
Membership
Volunteer Genealogists

Librarian
Literacy Promotion
Women's Issues

Historian
Chapter History Book Sales
Chapter Historian

NSDAR MISSION STATEMENT
The mission of the National Society Daughters
of the American Revolution is to promote
historic preservation, education and patriotism

MEMBERS AND NEW HORIZONS COURSES

Are you a new member? Has it been a few years since you have been active and you are looking for a DAR refresher? Members interested can register for the "Members Course" offered through the Illinois State Organization. As a note, anyone taking the course also needs to be an *American Spirit* magazine subscriber. Our Members Course Coordinator is Lucy Kron - she can be emailed at l_kron@msn.com

Member Course Graduates:
Lydia Roll (2017)
Courtenay Wood (2017)
B.A. Church (2018)
Stephanie Neilitz (2018)
Nichole Swafford (2018)
Lisa Fox (2019)
Saundra Shelley (2019)

WHAT IS THE NEW HORIZONS COURSE?
Taking the next step and venturing out to explore new opportunities is what the New Horizons Course is all about. The course is designed for interested, enthusiastic, dedicated members to help develop them into future chapter and state leaders. Without leaders, no organization can be successful. It is the goal of the New Horizons Course to inspire and instill confidence in Daughters to take that next step into leadership.

The course is ideal for aspiring chapter and state leaders and consists of a series of online webinars, a study of DAR published resources, in-person activities, and a capstone project. Our New Horizons Course Coordinator is Lucy Kron - she can be emailed at l_kron@msn.com As a note, anyone taking the course also needs to be an *American Spirit* magazine subscriber.

New Horizons Course Graduates
Julia Riley Davila (2017)
Courtenay Wood (2017)
B.A. Church (2018)
Stephanie Neilitz (2018)
Lydia Roll (2019)

2018 CHAPTER AWARDS

IL State Awards

Dawn Edwards - Women's Issues Essay Contest
Sharon Peterson - Women's Issues Essay Contest
Lisa Fox- Women's Issues Essay Contest
Nichole Swafford - Outstanding Chaplain Efforts
Nichole Swafford - Chapter Outstanding Junior
Chapter Development and Revitalization Commission Award -
Chicago Chapter for Debbie Duay Workshops

National Awards

Chapter Achievement Award Level I
Constitution Week Leadership Award - Chapter
Outstanding Recruitment and New Member Efforts
Outstanding Use of Social Media for Public Relations
Margaret Becker - Outstanding Correspondent Docent

CHILDREN OF THE AMERICAN REVOLUTION SOCIETY

The Chicago Chapter NSDAR sponsors a Children of the American Revolution Society (C.A.R.), the Mary Virginia Ellet Cabell Society.

The National Society of the Children of the American Revolution trains young people in citizenship, leadership and love for America and its heritage. The goal of the Children of the American Revolution Committee is to provide leadership, guidance and support to C.A.R. members as they grow into responsible citizens.

DAR members who are 22 years of age or older have the opportunity to play an active role as senior leaders for C.A.R. The experience of mentoring a young person and seeing them develop self-confidence and leadership is one of life's most rewarding experiences.

Please contact Julia Davila Riley at julia.riley.dar@gmail.com

2019-2020 CHICAGO
CHAPTER PROGRAM CALENDAR

September 7, 2019 | Chicago Chapter DAR Genealogy Workshop
11:00 a.m. Newberry Library

September 14, 2019 | DAR Day – Meeting and Workshops
9:00 a.m. (Registration at 8 a.m.)
DAR Days – Meeting and Workshops
Location: Sheraton Lisle/Naperville: 3000 Warrenville Road, Lisle, IL 60532

September 17 - 23, 2019 | Constitution Week

September 21, 2019 | September Chapter Meeting
Networking: 10:00 a.m.
Business Meeting: 10:30 a.m.
Program: 10:45 a.m. "The Role of Photographing Tombstones in Preserving Family Lineage"- Program by Sharon Zingery, Chapter Chaplain and Lineage Research Chair.
Location: Woman's Athletic Club - 626 N. Michigan Avenue
In-kind Donation: Art & Craft supplies and cards with patriotic theme
Mission: Historic Preservation / Patriotism

September 30, 2019 | Annual Membership Fees Are Due
Dues paid after October 1, 2019 incur a $10 late fee.

October 5, 2019 | Chicago Chapter DAR Genealogy Workshop
11:00 a.m. Newberry Library

October 12 , 2019 | National DAR Day of Service
Findagrave.com project at Graceland Cemetery in Chicago. Contact Sharon Zingery at szingery@gmail.com or 773-262-7699 or Misty Deckard at gryphon7378@gmail.com for details.

October 12 - 19 , 2019 | Illinois DAR Schools Bus Tour
Illinois Daughters will travel to Hindman Settlement in Kentucky, Crossnore School in North Carolina, Tamassee DAR School in South Carolina, Berry College in Rome, Georgia, and Kate Duncan Smith School in Alabama.

October 19, 2020 | Honoring and Supporting Chicago Teachers
Networking: 10:00 a.m.
Business Meeting: 10:30 a.m.
Program: 10:45 a.m. "The Single Woman in US History" presented by Susan Elliott, 2018 Newberry Teacher Fellowship Winner
Location: Woman's Athletic Club - 626 N. Michigan Avenue
In-kind Donation: Active Troop Care Kits
Mission: Education

October 25, 2019 | Make the Case Literacy Event

November 1, 2019 | District IV Meeting
Location: Carlisle Banquets, 435 E Butterfield Rd, Lombard, IL
Doors open 8:30 a.m. — Meeting starts 9:30 a.m.
Veteran emphasis — bring socks, hats, etc. for Standdown

November 2, 2019 | Chicago Chapter DAR Genealogy Workshop
11:00 a.m. Newberry Library

November 9, 2019 | November Chapter Meeting
Networking: 10:00 a.m.
Eagle Staff Presentation 10:30 a.m. Trickster Gallery
Business Meeting: 10:40 a.m.
Program: 11:15 a.m. D-DAY Commemoration presented by Dom Errichiello, a surviving D-Day veteran.
Location: Woman's Athletic Club - 626 N. Michigan Avenue
In-kind Donation: Trickster Gallery School Tour Art Program
Mission: Patriotism / American Indians / Literacy Promotion

December 7, 2019 | Chicago Chapter DAR Genealogy Workshop
11:00 a.m. Newberry Library

December 14, 2019 | Jesse Brown Holiday Party
Membership Activity: 10:00 a.m.
Bingo with the Veterans: 11:00 a.m. Bingo with the Veterans
Location: Jesse Brown VA Medical Center, 820 S. Damen, Chicago, IL
Donation: Canteen Books
Mission: Patriotism / Service for Veterans

January 4, 2020 | Chicago Chapter DAR Genealogy Workshop
11:00 a.m. Newberry Library

January 18, 2020 | Semiannual Business Meeting
Networking: 10:00 a.m.
Business Meeting: 10:30 a.m. Officer and Committee Reports
Location: Woman's Athletic Club - 626 N. Michigan Avenue
In-Kind Donation: Valentines and Care Kits
Mission: Membership

February 1, 2020 | Chicago Chapter DAR Genealogy Workshop
11:00 a.m. Newberry Library

February 22, 2020 | State Regents Program and George Washington's Birthday Celebration
State Regent, Sharla Luken will present her program "Serving Those Who Have Served Us"
Receiving Line and Social: 10:00 a.m.
Business Meeting: 10:30 a.m.
Program: 10:45 a.m.
Location: Woman's Athletic Club - 626 N. Michigan Avenue
Mission: Commemorative Events / DAR Service for Veterans

March 7, 2020 | Chicago Chapter DAR Genealogy Workshop
11:00 a.m. Newberry Library

March 6, 2020 | District IV Meeting
Youth Essay Contest
Location: Carlisle Banquets, 435 E Butterfield Rd, Lombard, IL
Doors open 8:30 a.m. — Meeting starts 9:30 a.m.

March 21, 2019 | Honoring and Supporting Chicago's Female Veterans
Networking: 10:00 a.m.
Business Meeting: 10:30 a.m.
Program: 11:30 a.m. "VA Women's Services" presented by Jenny Sitzer, Jesse Brown VA
Location: Woman's Athletic Club - 626 N. Michigan Avenue
In-kind Donation: Chicago Standdown Women's Care Kits
Mission: Women's Issues / DAR Service for Veterans

April 4, 2020 | Chicago Chapter DAR Genealogy Workshop
11:00 a.m. Newberry Library

April 18, 2020 | Historical Education
Networking: 10:00 a.m.
Business Meeting: 10:30 a.m.
Program: 10:45 a.m. "The American Revolution: Beyond the Battlefield" by Karen Chase, Author and DAR Member
Location: Woman's Athletic Club - 626 N. Michigan Avenue
In-kind Donation: Recycling Program
Mission: Education / Conservation

April 24-26, 2020 | Illinois DAR State Conference
DoubleTree Hotel, Bloomington, IL

May 2, 2020 | Chicago Chapter DAR Genealogy Workshop
11:00 a.m. Newberry Library

May 16, 2020 | Annual Business Meeting
Networking: 10:00 a.m.
Business Meeting and Awards Ceremony: 10:30 a.m.
Installation of Officers 11:00 a.m.
Memorial Service: 11:00 a.m.
Program: 11:30 a.m. "From a Box of Stuff, a Lincoln Connection" program given by Ellen Peirce, Chicago Chapter Member and Author
Location: Woman's Athletic Club - 626 N. Michigan Avenue
In-kind Donation: School Supplies
Mission: Membership / Education

June 6, 2020 | Chicago Chapter DAR Genealogy Workshop
11:00 a.m. Newberry Library

June 5, 2020 | District Meeting & Mini Tour
Honoring Past District Directors
Location: Carlisle Banquets, 435 E Butterfield Rd., Lombard, IL
Doors open 8:30 a.m. — Meeting starts 9:30 a.m.
Bring socks, hats, etc. for Standdown

June 20, 2020 | Chapter Planning Meeting
Networking: 10:00 a.m.
Business Meeting: 10:30 a.m.
Community Service Fair: 11:00 a.m.
Location: Woman's Athletic Club - 626 N. Michigan Avenue

June 24-28, 2020 | DAR Continental Congress
Location: Washington, DC. The IL Supper is June 23, 2020

ABOUT CHAPTER MEETINGS
Chapter meetings are generally held on the third Saturday of each month at 10:00 a.m. (unless otherwise scheduled). Please check the preceding pages of this yearbook for the times and locations of meetings. Details and updates are sent in advance of each meeting in email newsletters from thefirstchapter@darchicago.org.

The meetings are structured as follows:

10:00 a.m. - 10:30 a.m. Networking
10:30 a.m. - 12:00 p.m. Meeting and Program
Each regular chapter meeting includes an invocation, the DAR Ritual for meetings, committee reports, and an engaging program.

Committee Meetings
Committees are welcome to schedule meetings at 9:30 a.m. the day of a chapter meeting, before the meeting begins.

Volunteer Genealogists | Genealogy Workshops
Held monthly at the Newberry Library, these workshops begin with the Newberry's orientation of the their local history and genealogy collections All members, associates, prospectives and friends are welcome. The workshop is intended for new applicants to work on their application with a volunteer from the genealogical team. Members are also welcome to work on their supplemental applications and receive aid.

Junior Membership | Events for Members & Prospective Members
Junior Membership (for women ages 18-35) offers additional events, fund raisers and opportunities to get involved. They post their information regularly. All members, associates, prospectives and friends are welcome to attend events hosted by the Junior committee.

Membership| Pop-Up Events
These get-togethers have a short RSVP time, but offer a spectrum of opportunities to meet people. The events vary so there is something for everyone. All members, associates, prospectives and friends are welcome.

Membership | Bertha Honoré Palmer New Member's Tea
Approximately 2 - 3 times a year — Details are sent via chapter email before each event.

REGISTRATION/MEAL DETAILS FOR CHAPTER DISTRICT MEETINGS AND EVENTS

DISTRICT IV MEETINGS & LUNCHEONS – Reservations and payment are due approximately two weeks in advance. All checks should be made out to the hostess chapter and mailed to them directly. Meeting details and hostess chapter will be announced in the newsletter. Presently the cost for each District IV luncheon is $28.00.

If you would like to subscribe to the quarterly District IV Newsletter, please contact **illinois4thdistrictdar@gmail.com**.

CHAPTER LUNCHEONS or TEAS
Reservations and payment are due no later than one week prior.

Some dietary requests may be accommodated. The costs will be announced via newsletter. Checks and PayPal are accepted.

Note: We politely ask for RSVPs to all events so we can plan accordingly. The chapter RSVP email is **rsvp@darchicago.org**

DAR RITUAL FOR MEETINGS & EVENTS

The Pledge of Allegiance
I pledge allegiance to the flag
of the United States of America
and to the Republic for which it stands,
one Nation under God, indivisible,
with liberty and justice for all.

Francis Bellamy

The American's Creed
I believe in the United States of America as a government of the people,
by the people, for the people; whose just powers are derived from the
consent of the governed; a democracy in a republic; a sovereign Nation of
many sovereign states; a perfect Union, one and inseparable,
established upon those principles of freedom, equality, justice and
humanity for which American patriots sacrificed their lives and fortunes.
I therefore believe it is my duty to my country to love it; to support its
Constitution; to obey its laws; to respect its flag, and to defend it against
all enemies.

William Tyler Page

Chicago Chapter Benediction
May the patriotism and loyalty of our ancestors; their faith in this
country; and their hope for peace; continue in our minds and hearts
making for the highest ideals of this Chicago Chapter, and of the
country in which we live.

Blanche C. Murray (Mrs. Willis Grant)

CHAPTER MEMBERS

#Chicago Chapter Life Member   + Life Member   ☻ Past Regent   *Junior Member

920677   Alfonso, Penelope Anne Smith (Mrs. Benjamin)
4900 N. Marine Dr. Apt. 411   H: (818) 317-7020
Chicago, IL 60640-3961   Birthday: May 27
palfonso48@yahoo.com   Admitted: June 24, 2013
William Lazell, VT, Pvt

919537   Alger, Sarah Jeanette
152 N. Main Street, Apt. 2E   Birthday: Oct. 28
Concord, NH 03301-8921   Admitted: June 24, 2013
sarah.alger.dar@gmail.com
Richard Taylor, VA, LCol; James Alger, MA, Pvt

932967   Altman, Cara Elizabeth*
3603 N. Janssen Ave. Apt. 3   H: (718) 644-2572
Chicago, IL 60613-3707   Birthday: July 22
cara.altman@gmail.com   Admitted: June 5, 2014
Edmund Bugg, GA, CS PS

897231   Anderson, Eve Alice
521 Lake Ave.   H: (847) 323-2997
Wilmette, IL 60091-2607   Birthday: May 1
eaa419@hotmail.com   Admitted: Oct. 8, 2011
Johan Conrad Kershner, Jr, PA, PS

882326   Ary, Suzanne Lynn
411 22nd St.   H: (773) 278-2903
Virginia Beach, VA 23451-3379   Birthday: Oct.19
Sary@mzb-usa.com   Admitted: July 5, 2010
Adam Brown, PA, Pvt

920455   Bach, Elizabeth King Ingle (Mrs. Bernard Raymond, Jr.)
1029 Franklin Ave.   H: (708) 771-2941
River Forest, IL 60305-1339   Birthday: Dec. 20
elizabeth.i.bach@gmail.com   Admitted: June 24, 2013
Henry Bohanon, VA, Pvt

889064 **Bagley, Mary Kirkendall**
1300 N. State Pkwy. Apt. 901   H: (312) 867-1954
Chicago, IL 60610-8657   Birthday: Sept 29
mary.bagley@comcast.net   Admitted: Dec. 11, 2010
William Hammond, RI, CS PS

892129 **Ballerini, Janet Susan Ary (Mrs. Joseph Michael)**
505 Misty Creek Dr.   Birthday: Sept 13
New Lenox, IL 60451-3316   Admitted: April 9, 2011
janet.ballerini@gmail.com
Adam Brown, PA, Pvt

966495 **Bankard, Susan Jane Turner (Mrs. James Howard)**
716 W. Hutchinson St.   H: (773) 398-7145
Chicago, IL 60613-1520   Birthday: Feb. 20
bankard.susan@gmail.com   Admitted: March 5, 2017
Mathew Terrell, VA, Noncom

878663 **Bartholomew, Kristen Janel**
1650 Buttonwood Cir. Apt. 3125   H: (773) 206-3481
Schaumburg, IL 60173-6207   Birthday: Dec. 11
kristenchicago@gmail.com   Admitted: Feb. 6, 2010
Daniel Bartholomew, PA, Pvt

963551 **Barton, Cynthia Catherine**
153 Lafayette Ave. Apt. 2   H: (718) 208-6894
Brooklyn, NY 11238-1075   Birthday: Feb. 15
cynthia.barton@gmail.com   Admitted: Nov. 5, 2016
George Wenner, PA, Noncom

994098 **Baumgarten, Martha Spreuer***
2329 W. Shakespeare Ave.   Birthday: Oct.29
Chicago, IL 60647-3218   Admitted: May 5, 2019
marion.baumgarten41@gmail.com
Thomas Owsley, Sr, VA, PS

763086   Becker, Margaret Ann (Mrs. John Lee)
1333 Maple Ave. Apt. 2D   H: (847) 905-0211
Evanston, IL 60201-4387   Birthday: Nov. 25
peggyann60126@yahoo.com   Admitted: Dec.7, 1994
James Armstrong, PA, Pvt; Philip Forney, PA, PS;
Adam Diller, PA, Pvt ; Adam Diller, Jr, PA, Pvt;
Adam Diller, Sr, PA, Pvt; Casper Elias Diller, PA, PS;
David Stansbury, MD, Pvt PS; Thomas Stansbury, MD, PS

983899   Bentley, Cintra de Noyelles
100 E. 14th St. Apt. 2404   H: (773) 339-3382
Chicago, IL 60605-3674   Birthday: Aug. 10
cdbentley@outlook.com   Admitted: Aug. 5, 2018
John Felter, NY, Pvt

879358   Bernardini, Roe Chase
2835 N. Sheffield Ave. Ste. 224   C: (773) 975-1166
Chicago, IL 60657-5083   Birthday: June 26
roebernsw@gmail.com   Admitted: Feb. 6, 2010
Paul Chase, RI, Pvt

943656   Bernhard-Rhone, Lauren Ann (Mrs. Ross Hugh)
1211 W. 33rd Pl.   H: (773) 843-0964
Chicago, IL 60608-6459   Birthday: Nov. 2
lauren.rhone@gmail.com   Admitted: May 5, 2015
Innett Hollister, CT & VT, Pvt

923964   Betchner, Robyn Marie
1201 S. Prairie Ave. Apt. 1005   H: (312) 519-5912
Chicago, IL 60605-3422   Birthday: July 30
rmbetchner@gmail.com   Admitted: Oct. 5, 2013
Benjamin Braswell, NC, CS

942279   Bigwood, Joanne Elizabeth OMalley (Mrs. John Miller)
7719 E. Prairie Rd.   H: (847) 779-3053
Skokie, IL 60076-3633   Birthday: June 28
johnbigwood84@gmail.com   Admitted: April 5, 2015
Thomas Sanford, CT, Pvt

882264 **Bodine, Pegeen Luzon Wood** **(Mrs. Paul Arthur)**
1819 N. Lincoln Park W.   H: (312) 649-9176
Chicago, IL 60614-7975   Birthday: May 29
pbodine@contactoffice.com   Admitted: July 5, 2010
Moses Congleton, PA, Noncom

874010 **Boice, Heather Ann**
3311 Graylock Run   Birthday: Oct. 8
Broomfield, CO 80023-8040   Admitted: July 6, 2009
haboice@yahoo.com
John Emery, NJ, PS ; Nehemiah Sprague, MA, Cpl; Leonard Pike, MA & VT, Pvt CS ; Samuel Houston, NC, Sol ; Shubael Luce, NJ, Sol ; Lemuel Brooks, CT, Sol ; Benjamin Jenney, MA, Sgt ; Thomas Barber, VA, PS ; Jonathan Smith, MA, Col CS PS; Benanuel Salisbury, NY, Pvt.; Gideon Salisbury, NY, PS; John Bassett, MA, Pvt.; Barbara BRACKBILL Groff, PA, PS ; Collins Ludington, CT, Pvt. CS; John Groff, PA, PS; Elijah Smith, CT, CS; John Sherman, MA, CS; Hattil Kelly, MA, CS; Stukeley Sayles, RI, Pvt; Uriah Alverson, RI, CS PS ; Richard Sayles, RI, CS ; Asa Freeman, MA, CS ; Silas Hewitt, CT & RI, Pvt ; Silvanus Stevens, CT, Pvt ; Solomon Cortright, NJ, Sgt; Christian Furr, PA, PS ; Frances X Herr, PA, PS ; George Delshaver, VA, PS ; Job Larcom, CT, PS

722872 **Bornhoeft, Linda Ann Wickless** **(Mrs. James Stephan)**
33 Drexel Ave.   H: (708) 579-0426
La Grange, IL 60525-5815   Birthday: Nov. 13
jlbornhoeft@gmail.com   Admitted: June 2, 1989
John Marshall, VA, Capt

810887 **Bouck, Phyllis Henrietta Culp** **(Mrs. David William)**
13134 Avenida La Valencia   H: (858) 485-7727
Poway, CA 92064-1906   Birthday: Jan. 31
pbsinbachs@aol.com   Admitted: April 13, 2002
Robert Snow, Sr, CT, Sol

933499 **Brennan, Mary Christine***
906 W. Wrightwood Ave. Apt. 2   H: (312) 610-0119
Chicago, IL 60614-6171   Birthday: April 10
mcbrennan2@gmail.com   Admitted: July 5, 2014
Peletiah Fitch, NY, Lt PS

997601 Brunson, Jamie Lee
2004 N. Clifton Ave. Apt. A   H: (312) 757-0252
Chicago, IL 60614-4120   Birthday: Aug. 24
jamiebrunson@gmail.com   Admitted: August 5, 2019
Joseph Simmons, MA-CT, Pvt

900076 Brinsmade, Anne Hudson
3270 N. Lake Shore Dr. Apt. 6D   H: (410) 610- 6209
Chicago, IL 60657-3921   Birthday: March 12
abrinsmade@yahoo.com   Admitted: Dec. 10, 2011
Abraham Brinsmade, CT, Capt CS PS

669610 Buckley, Patricia Logsdon (Mrs. John Lawrence, Jr)
6314 S. Albany Ave.   H: (773) 434-6633
Chicago, IL 60629-2728   Birthday: July 17
patbuckley39@comcast.net   Admitted: Feb. 4, 1983
Abraham Spitler, VA, Pvt PS

Burns, Meg Elizabeth Quigley
1101 S. State St. Apt. 507   H: (847) 302-1887
Chicago, IL 60605-3177
megyver2@gmail.com

572042 Burke, Jeanne W Smith (Mrs. James P)
3225 Brookdale Ln.   H: (847) 302-5572
Northbrook, IL 60062-7501   Birthday: Oct. 13
burkecinq50@yahoo.com   Admitted: Oct.13, 1972
Gamaliel Parker, Jr, CT, Pvt PS

895582 Burrell, Vicki Replogle (Mrs. Timothy Richard)
P.O. Box 20   H: (312) 929-7409
Hesperia, MI 49421-0020   Birthday: June 1
vicki.burrell@att.net   Admitted: Oct. 8, 2011
Rinehart Replogle, Sr, PA, Pvt; John Phillip Replogle, MD, PS

935692 Calore, Patricia Fraser Wyche (Mrs. Jeffrey)
2715 N. Pine Grove Ave. #3   H: (703) 327-1656
Chicago, IL 60614-6109   Birthday: June 26
pfcalore@yahoo.com   Admitted: Sept. 5, 2014
Richard Henry Lee, VA, Col PS SDI

876095 **Carden, Nancy Virginia Stasiak (Mrs. Carl Ernest)**
1730 Avenida De Mundo #505   H: (619) 213-4050
Coronado, CA 92118   Birthday: April 12
ccarden@san.rr.com   Admitted: Oct. 3, 2009
Moses Dalton, VA, Sgt

330612 **Carlson, Margaret Deffenbaugh (Mrs. Leroy Theodore)**
2 Milburn Park   H: (847) 864-4345
Evanston, IL 60201-1744   Admitted: Dec. 17, 1941
medcarlson@aol.com   Birthday: Jan. 20
John George Diefenbaugh, PA, Ens ; Walter Watson, MD, Pvt

557135 **Carlson, Prudence Elizabeth**
17 White St. # 6B   H: (212) 966-1210
New York, NY 10013-2447   Birthday: July 13
sans_souci@earthlink.net   Admitted: Feb. 1, 1971
John George Diefenbaugh, PA, Ens

897453 **Chait, Mary Elizabeth Lardner**
1325 N. State Pkwy. Apt. 11F   H: (312) 961-4404
Chicago, IL 60610-6120   Birthday: June 13
marychait@gmail.com   Admitted: Oct. 8, 2011
Thomas Bedford, Jr, VA, Lt

873708 **Charnowski, Elizabeth Danford***
1241 W. Oakdale   C: (314) 800-4419
Chicago, IL 60657   Birthday: Nov. 21
echarnowski@gmail.com   Admitted: July 6, 2009
Peter Danforth, NJ, Sol

980939 **Christopher, Rebecca Lyn**
400 E. Randolph St. Apt. 1715   H: (312) 315-6500
Chicago, IL 60601-7306   Birthday: Sept. 28
revkka@aol.com   Admitted: May 5, 2018
Moses Evans, NJ, PS

677653 Church, B. A. ✪
2321 W. Berwyn Ave.
Chicago, IL 60625-1120
bachurch1@juno.com
Lewis Day, MA, Sgt ; Timothy Day, MA, CS ;
Peter Mason, CT, CS PS; James Sappington, PA, Pvt;
Richard Wells, Sr, VA & PA, PS

H: (773) 989-8407
Birthday: Aug. 22
Admitted: Oct. 14, 1983

970865 Cicak, Sarah Nevada
1720 S. Michigan Ave. Apt. 2205
Chicago, IL 60616-4854
sarah.cicak@gmail.com
Samuel Sackett, CT & PA, Staff Of

H: (208) 371-2293
Birthday: Oct. 20
Admitted: July 5, 2017

789226 Clarke, Nancy Marple ✪ **(Mrs. James)**
3449 W. 76th Pl.
Chicago, IL 60652-1407
marpnj@gmail.com
Benjamin Clark, NJ, Pvt CS; Jacob Fisler, Jr, NJ, Pvt;
Richard Cheesman, NJ, Capt; Jacob Fisler, Sr, NJ, PS

H: (773) 203-7012
Birthday: March 15
Admitted: Feb 6, 1999

903060 Cochran, Susan Kay
1316 W. Nelson St.
Chicago, IL 60657
skaycochran@me.com
Reuben Landon, CT, Pvt

H: (847) 867-9947
Birthday: March 25
Admitted: April 21, 2012

880882 Combs, Brittany Michelle*
840 W Blackhawk St, Apt. 1404
Chicago, IL 60642
brit.combs@gmail.com
James Harkness, MA, Sgt

Birthday: May 19
Admitted: April 17, 2010

877112 Cornell, Nancy
5060 N. Marine Dr. Apt C7
Chicago, IL 606640-3273
nac1200@ol.com
Noadiah Dickinson, NJ, Pvt

H: (773) 728-7945
Birthday: June 9
Admitted: Dec. 12, 2009

869135 Corral, Nancy Ann Raymond
1242 N. Lake Shore Dr. # 23   H: (312) 867-1801
Chicago, IL 60610-2332   Birthday: Jan. 22
ncorral@sbcglobal.net   Admitted: Feb. 7, 2009
Jacob Story, MA, Lt

993663 Covell, Barbara Ann
620 W. Briar Pl. Apt. 2R   H: (312) 622-2463
Chicago, IL 60657-4521   Birthday: March 16
covell.barbara@sbcglobal.net   Admitted: May 5, 2019
Thomas Loomis, CT, Capt

749872 Cramsie, Marion Josephine Samuelson (Mrs. James Francis)
1300 N. Lake Shore Dr. Apt. 3C   H: (312) 280-8529
Chicago, IL 60610-2157   Birthday: July 8
marionj78@gmail.com   Admitted: Dec. 9, 1992
Robert Snow, Sr, CT, Sol ; Levin Hurley, DE, Cpl;
Ross Crosley, PA, Pvt PS

870113 Crews, Cara Marie Heber*
5042 N. Oak Park Ave.   H: (847) 903-5977
Chicago, IL 60656-3740   Birthday: May 20
caraheber@gmail.com   Admitted: April 25, 2009
Abraham Granger, Sr, CT, Pvt PS

565811 Curtis, Heather Valerie Hunley (Mrs. Kenneth)
19898 County Highway A   H: (608) 965-3183
Shullsburg, WI 53586   Birthday: Dec. 1
heathercurtis@gmail.com   Admitted: Feb. 1, 1972
Daniel Solsbee, PA, Pvt

915211 Davila, Julia Ann Riley (Mrs. Igor)
3437 N. Janssen Ave. # 2   H: (314)707-1532
Chicago, IL 60657-1321   Birthday: June 1
julia.riley.dar@gmail.com   Admitted: Feb. 2, 2013
John Crandall, RI, Pvt

992780 **Deckard, Misty Renee**
550 W. Surf St.   H: (312) 561-3409
Chicago, IL 60657-6036   Birthday: April 29
gryphon7378@gmail.com   Admitted: April 5, 2019
William Gregory, NC, Pvt

909795 **Deitrick, Emily Jane Posey (Mrs. William Edgar)**
70 E. Cedar St # 6W   H: (312) 587-0081
Chicago, IL 60611-1179   Birthday: July 25
epdeitr@aol.com   Admitted: Oct. 6, 2012
Micajah Posey, PA, Pvt PS; Isaac Mchenry, PA, Lt

881728 **Dismang, Mary Genva Carver (Mrs. Robert Glen)**
5221 N. Long Ave.   H: (773) 286-8677
Chicago, IL 60630-1437   Birthday: Aug. 15
mgdismang@sbcglobal.net   Admitted: April 17, 2010
Abraham Hayter, MD & VA, Capt CS

917832 **Donovan, Deanna Jean De Christopher (Mrs. Michael)**
7718 Walinca Ter.   H: (314) 932-7433
Clayton, MO 63105-2042   Birthday: Nov. 7
mtddjd07@gmail.com   Admitted: April 13, 2013
Samuel Stoddard, MA, Pvt

904434 **Doyle, Ashley**
1344 Greenwillow Ln. Unit 1W
Glenview, IL 60025-5527
ashleydoyle8@gmail.com   Admitted: April 2012
John Adams, NH, CS, PS

875554 **Dravillas, Jenifer Anne Spreitzer (Mrs. Speleos George)**
1030 N. State St. Unit 10EF   H: (312) 925-4222
Chicago, IL 60610-5476   Birthday: Aug. 6
jendravillas@yahoo.com   Admitted: Oct. 3, 2009
Thomas Pettus, Sr, VA, CS PS

973456 **Dudek, Benjalyn Elaine Harris (Mrs. Charles Richard)**
10741 Bunker Hwy.   H: (517) 663-4190
Eaton Rapids, MI 48827-9335   Birthday: Sept. 11
benjalynedudek@yahoo.com   Admitted: Oct 5, 2017
George Van Der Veer, VA, Pvt

920238 **Dudek, Debra Marguerite**
8 Merrimack Ct.
Bolingbrook, IL 60440-1461
debradudek@yahoo.com
Isaiah Ward, NJ, Pvt

H: (231) 920-6313
Birthday: April 2
Admitted: June 24, 2013

952961 **Dudek, Kristin Marie**
355 E. Ohio St. Unit 1908
Chicago, IL 60611-5593
kdudekrdh@yahoo.com
Isaiah Ward, NJ, Pvt

H: (616) 292-8720
Birthday: Jan. 28
Admitted: Jan. 5, 2016

904342 **Dufour, Stina Marie Peterson (Mrs. John David)***
395 Stratford Rd. Apt. A3
Brooklyn, NY 11218-5361
stina.dufour@gmail.com
Ephraim Wilson, MA, Pvt PS

H: (773) 465-2189
Birthday: Aug. 24
Admitted: April 21, 2012

898962 **Duvall, Katherine**
9300 S. Bell
Chicago, IL 60643
duvall@uic.edu
Samuel Braley, RI, Cp

Birthday: Oct. 30
Admitted: Dec 10, 2011

967767 **Edsey, Katherine Byrne Keating (Mrs. David Joseph)**
4003 N. Kenmore Ave. Apt. G
Chicago, IL 60613-2465
k_keatingedsey@yahoo.com
James Cassidy, VA, Pvt

H: (773) 294-6329
Birthday: Nov. 7
Admitted: April 5, 2017

956026 **Edwards, Dawn Ann**
1 Nevada Plz Apt. 9H
New York, NY 10023-5021
DAE2100@yahoo.com
Julius Chancellor, VA, Pvt

C: (312) 266-3350
Birthday: Jan. 13
Admitted: April 5, 2016

979277 **Ellsworth, Martha Louise**
2626 N. Lakeview Ave. Apt. 2304
Chicago, IL 60614-1814
marymariah29@gmail.com
Aaron Pratt, MA, Pvt

H: (773) 929-0997
Birthday: June 30
Admitted: March 5, 2018

973455 Elwell, Betty Geneva Sims (Mrs. Rondell H.)
205A Unicoi St.   Birthday: Feb. 22
Helen, GA 30545-3103   Admitted: Oct. 5, 2017
George Van Der Veer, VA, Pvt

604295 Engler, Pamela Ann Hunley (Mrs. Vincent)
6332 205th Ave.
Bristol, WI 53104-9730   Birthday: Aug. 22
pamelaengler@yahoo.com   Admitted: Jan. 30, 1976
Daniel Solsbee, PA, Pvt

872848 Farr, Ellen Marie*
600 N. McClurg Ct. Apt. 4112
Chicago, IL 60611-6935   Birthday: Nov. 7
ellie.farr@gmail.com   Admitted: July 6, 2009
Nathan Salisbury, RI, Pvt

990344 Fine, Natalie Anne*
14 W. Elm St. Apt. 203   H: (317) 697-8899
Chicago, IL 60610-2736   Birthday: March 22
natannefine@gmail.com   Admitted: Feb. 5, 2019
James Daugherty, PA, Pvt PS

673320 Fletcher, Sally
1443 S. Indiana Ave.   H: (312) 848-5400
Chicago, IL 60605-2834   Birthday: Dec. 30
sfletcher@fletch.com   Admitted: April 16, 1983
Moses Rugg, MA, Pvt

871976 Fluecke, Allison Whitney Heller (Mrs. Joshua James)
844 Carpenter Ave.   H: (708) 386-5385
Oak Park, IL 60304-1148   Birthday: May 16
afluecke@gmail.com   Admitted: April 25, 2009
John Ten Broeck, NJ, LCol

956737 Fornari, Erica Christine
900 S. Clark St. Apt. 1016   H: (202) 236-9144
Chicago, IL 60605-3688   Birthday: April 24
efornari@gmail.com   Admitted: May 5, 2016
Joseph Talcott, CT, PS; Jonathan Hubbard, CT, PS

969091 **Fortune, Grace Evelyn Wright**
1310 N. Ritchie Ct. Apt. 16D   H: (860) 906-8812
Chicago, IL 60610-8401   Birthday: June 16
GWFortune@gmail.com   Admitted: May 5, 2017
William Hewitt, CT, Pvt ; Arthur Hewitt, NY, Pvt

968031 **Fox, Lisa Michelle White (Mrs. Timothy Walter)**
3314 Laurel Ln.   H: (708) 829-5565
Hazel Crest, IL 60429-1009   Birthday: Jan 21
lmfox29@hotmail.com   Admitted: April 5, 2017
Josiah Milton, VA, PS

933129 **Fuller, Morgan Elizabeth***
1825 W. Byron St. Unit 3   H: (256) 508-5880
Chicago, IL 60613-2729   Birthday: May 26
mef1247@gmail.com   Admitted: June 5, 2014
Israel Hubbard, Sr, MA, CS PS

902761 **Gavin , Martha Alexandra Conrad***
233 Middaugh Rd   H: (847) 644-3994
Clarendon Hills, IL 60514   Birthday: Mar. 13
mgavin313@gmail.com   Admitted: Feb. 4, 2012
William Brown, PA & VA, Pvt

992783 **George, Rebecca Ann**
4862 W. Warner Ave.   H: (773) 706-0079
Chicago, IL 60641-1818   Birthday: Dec. 9
rebeccageorge.darchicago@yahoo.com Admitted: April 5, 2019
Joshua Hadley, NC, PS

599915 **Gidwitz, Mary Kathryn Westfall (Mrs. James)**
1260 N. Astor St.   H: (312) 664-5559
Chicago, IL 60610-2308   Birthday: Mar. 24
Admitted: 17 Oct 1975
Pierre Savoie, LA, PS

896997 **Graves, Jamie Lynne**
2352 W. Wilson 1E   H: (309) 648-5689
Chicago, IL 60625   Birthday: May 11
jamiegraves@gmail.com   Admitted: Oct. 8, 2011
Bela Graves, CT, Pvt

884770 Gray, Laurel Dawn
275 Churchill Pl.
Clarendon Hills, IL 60514-1324
laurelg23@yahoo.com
Moses Porter, CT, Sgt

H: (312) 371-1810
Birthday: May 23
Admitted: Oct. 9, 2010

938738 Grimm, Marni*
4944 Shannamara Dr.
Matthews, NC 28104-2999
marni.grimm@gmail.com
Consider Lucas, MA, Pvt

Birthday: Aug.14
Admitted: Dec 5, 2014

908504 Hamlin, Sally Jo Torrance
3600 N. Lake Shore Dr. Apt. 314
Chicago, IL 60613-4655
salham61@gmail.com
John Kidd, VA, Sol

H: (513) 314-5442
Birthday: Aug. 31
Admitted: Oct. 6, 2012

871969 Hankins, Katherine Stasiak (Mrs. Jordan Henry)
P.O. Box 241962
Omaha, NE 68124-6962
kshankins@hotmail.com
Moses Dalton, VA, Sgt

H: (402) 393-1275
Birthday: Nov. 25
Admitted: April 25, 2009

810888 Hanna, Amanda Joy Bouck (Mrs. Matthew L)
2460 Eastbourne Dr.
Woodbridge, VA 22191-4062
titan4n6s@yahoo.com
Robert Snow, Sr, CT, Sol

H: (703) 910-6438
Birthday: June 12
Admitted: April 13, 2002

973459 Harris, Carsen Claire*
3881 Yellowstone Way SW
Lilburn, GA 30047-2585
simpamharris@comcast.net
George Van Der Veer, VA, Pvt

H: (770) 979-5742
Birthday: Nov. 19
Admitted: Oct. 5, 2017

952379 Hasenbeck-Meyer, Kaitlin
5118 S Ingleside "A"
Chicago, IL 60615
KSHASENBECK@gmail.com
James Johnston, VA, Sgt

H: (573) 353-9324
Birthday: Jan. 2
Admitted: Dec. 5, 2015

888606 Hayes, Laura Christine Jack
1145 W. Newport Ave. Unit T   H: (312) 721-3217
Chicago, IL 60657-1555   Birthday: April 2
laurajackhayes@gmail.com   Admitted: Dec. 11, 2010
Philip Grimes, VA, PS

547608 Healy, Jane Olt (Mrs. Thomas Hoyne)
625 W. Madison St. Apt. 606   C: (937) 789-1908
Chicago, IL 60661-2713   Birthday: Oct. 11
janihealy@gmail.com   Admitted: Jan. 31, 1970
John Mccoy, VA, Pvt

472602 Heck, Catherine Houser
P.O. Box 243   C: (312) 846-0029
Barrington, IL 60011-0243   Birthday: April 17
Admitted: April 16, 1960
Simon Shoemaker, PA, Pvt

997427 Heintzelman, Caroline
4609 W Patterson Ave   (703) 869-2474
Chicago, IL 60641-3610   Birthday: Sept. 3
Heintzelmance@gmail.com   Admitted: August 5, 2019
Collin McKenney, VA, CS

997426 Heintzelman, Patricia
N1529 Wildwood Rd   (262) 325-0403
Lake Geneva, WI 53147-4165   Birthday: March 7
lakegenevaartist@gmail.com   Admitted: August 5, 2019
Collin McKenney, VA, CS

967063 Henderson, Paula Ann Snorf (Mrs. Schuyler Kent)
The Old Mill, Upper Swell   H: (773) 818-2029
GL541EW Gloucestershire,   Birthday: May 13
United Kingdom   Admitted: March 5, 2017
henderson.paula@comcast.net
Henry Warner, PA, Pvt

976817   Hensel, Carol Ann
510 N. May St. Apt. 4R   H: (312) 373-1767
Chicago, IL 60642-5883   Member since:1/5/18
chensel3@comcast.net
Alexander Mack, PA, Pvt PS

895116   Hoganson, Mary Louise Rectenwald (Mrs. George Edward)
3525 S. Cass Ct. Unit 310   H: (312) 957-0966
Oak Brook, IL 60523-2697   Birthday: Aug. 26
maryhoganson@rcn.com   Admitted: June 27, 2011
John Van Bibber, VA, Capt

882258   Homola, Sandra Lynn
4408 N. Winchester Ave. Apt. 45   H: (773) 972-1907
Chicago, IL 60640-5853   Birthday: March 8
sandyhomola@hotmail.com   Admitted: July 5, 2010
George Lonas, VA, Pvt

937219   Honl Shannon
1809 W Argyle St Apt 1A   H: (608) 215-3695
Chicago, IL 60640   Birthday: June 15
shannon.honl@gmail.com   Admitted: Nov. 5, 2014
Amos Wade, MA, Capt

959740   Hood, Elizabeth Marie
5330 S. Hyde Park Blvd. Apt. 2S   H: (773) 332-6633
Chicago, IL 60615-5712   Birthday: Dec.18
liz.hood18@gmail.com   Admitted: Aug. 5, 2016
James Ellis, NY, Sol

706296   Howe, Louise
929 W. Foster Ave. Apt. 1705   H: (773) 561-5949
Chicago, IL 60640-1686   Birthday: Sept. 5
ldhowe@aol.com   Admitted: Feb. 6, 1987
James Brewster, VA, CS PS; Jabez Crosby, MA, Pvt PS;
Thomas Oldham, PA, Pvt

771622   **Humphrey, Janice May Gordon**
1846 W. Addison St.
Chicago, IL 60613-3503   H: (773) 975-9819
JHUMPLCSW@earthlink.net   Birthday: Dec. 5
Peter Tarter, NC & VA, Pvt   Admitted: June 8, 1996

937804   **Hurdelbrink, Elizabeth Libby***
2700 W. Belmont Ave.Unit 501
Chicago, IL 60618-5989   Birthday: Aug. 20
ehurdelbrink@gmail.com   Admitted: Nov. 5, 2014
Asa Walbridge, VT, Pvt

738412   **Huske, Mary Livingstone**
2211 S. Highland Ave. Apt. 2D   H: (630) 268-9851
Lombard, IL 60148-5348   Birthday: Sept.18
maryhuske@yahoo.com   Admitted: June 12, 1991
Joseph Bailey, MD, Pvt

900305   **Illian, Wendy Sue**
5057 N. Saint Louis Ave.   Birthday: May 10
Chicago, IL 60625-5528   Admitted: Dec. 10, 2011
wendy@brillantspaces.com
David Shriver, MD, LCol PS

920703   **Jacobs, Diana Lee Conway**
2028 W. Shakespeare Ave.   Birthday: May 2
Chicago, IL 60647-4535   Admitted: June 24, 2013
DJacobs1717@gmail.com
Gerardus Ryker, Sr, NJ, Ens

892601   **Janka, Diane Louise**
907 S. Kensington Ave   H: (240) 498-1009
La Grange, IL 60525-2712   Birthday: June 18
dwallendjack@gmail.com   Admitted: April 9, 2011
William Cary, MD, Pvt

617825   **Johnson, Judith Ann**
145 Heathrow Ct.   H: (847) 295-7959
Lake Bluff, IL 60044-1922   Birthday: Oct. 10
Admitted: Apr. 16, 1977
John Hoyt, Jr, MA, Cpl

906385 Johnson, Suzanne Holly
1350 N. Lake Shore Dr. Apt. 2201   H: (312) 607-2575
Chicago, IL 60610-5151   Birthday: Oct. 11
shjfsu@yahoo.com   Admitted: June 25, 2012
John Sparks, VA, PS

633650 Kasuboski, Robinette Vanessa Hunley (Mrs. Kenneth V)
7818 352nd Ave.   H: (262) 537-4237
Burlington, WI 53105-8848   Birthday: Dec. 16
fairwaytravel@wi.rr.com   Admitted: Dec. 13, 1978
Daniel Solsbee, PA, Pvt

871888 Kelly, Bennetta Elizabeth Pennisi (Mrs. Patrick)
2500 N. Lakeview Ave. Apt. 2103   C: (773) 580-9808
Chicago, IL 60614-4871   Birthday: Nov. 3
bennetta.kelly@gmail.com   Admitted: April 25, 2009
Philip Buckner, VA, Capt PS

884699 Kemp, Mary Campbell
1325 N. State Pkwy. Apt. 19C   H: (312) 337-6686
Chicago, IL 60610-2167   Birthday: Sept. 14
mcampbell007@ameritech.net   Admitted: Oct. 9, 2010
Uriah Whitney, CT, Pvt

880518 Keranen, Rachel Michelle
805 Hinman Ave. Apt. 2   H: (312) 772-5817
Evanston, IL 60202-5903   Birthday: Feb. 1
rachel.vajgrt@gmail.com   Admitted: April 17, 2010
James Brigham, VA & NC, CS PS

875471 King, Stephanie Tyner Mylenski*
1946 N. Howe St.   H: (312) 642-0581
Chicago, IL 60614-5128   Birthday: Aug. 26
stking@rcn.com   Admitted: Oct. 3, 2009
Joseph Palmer, CT, Capt

875470 King, Suzanne Marie Tyner (Mrs. Clark Chapman, III)
4301 Gulf Shore Blvd. N Apt. 502   H: (312) 642-0581
Naples, FL 34103   Birthday: Feb. 18
stking@rcn.com   Admitted: Oct. 3, 2009
Joseph Palmer, CT, Capt

979240 **Kiss, Gail Lee Ferguson (Mrs. Michael W.)**
1680 Overland Trl   H: (847) 337-0367
Deerfield, IL 60015-1810   Birthday: Sept 20
Kiss.gail@gmail.com   Admitted: March 5, 2018
Theodore King, CT, Pvt

995934 **Klein, Kathryn Leigh McGrath (Mrs. Jason Evan)**
2621 N. Wilson Avenue #3   H: (347) 907-0155
Chicago, IL 60614-2320   Birthday: June 22
ktnmcgrath@gmail.com   Admitted: July 5, 2019
William Sproul, MA, PS

878703 **Knizner, Amy Lynn Kalnasy (Mrs. Robert Thomas)***
14006 Meadow Ln.   H: (440) 829-7156
Plainfield, IL 60544-2886   Birthday: July 30
aknizner@gmail.com   Admitted: Feb. 6, 2010
William Talley, Sr, DE, Pvt

698261 **Koch, Raye Howells (Mrs. Paul Nathan)**
P.O. Box 251588   H: (408) 368-2573
Plano, TX 75025-1509   Birthday: Aug. 14
rayekochpt@hotmail.com   Admitted: Feb.7, 1986
John Middleswart, NJ, Noncom

952042 **Konicek, Alison Taylor (Mrs. Matthew Koei)***
4550 N. Maplewood Ave. Unit 1514   H: (352) 216-0674
Chicago, IL 60625   Birthday: Aug.19
at.jefferson6@gmail.com   Admitted: Dec. 5, 2015
Peter Denny, MD, Ens PS

989252 **Kron, Lucy Ellen**
1728 W. Terra Cotta Pl. Apt. D   H: (773) 975-8151
Chicago, IL 60614-1992   Birthday: Nov. 29
L_Kron@msn.com   Admitted: Feb. 5, 2019
Seth Chandler, CT, Sgt

971353 **Laczkowski, Tiffany Jane Gray (Mrs. Tobi Jay)**
726 9th St.   H: (224) 688-5463
Wilmette, IL 60091-2616   Birthday: Dec. 22
tiffany.laczkowski@gmail.com   Admitted: Aug. 5, 2017
Benjamin Van De Mark, PA, Pvt PS

938585 Lal, Ann Kellogg (Mrs. Anuj)
2253 W. Melrose St.   H: (309) 255-8810
Chicago, IL 60618   Birthday: Jan. 20
annkellogg7@gmail.com   Admitted: Dec 5, 2014
William Ramsay, PA, L

819168 Lane-Schmitz, Tara Joan (Mrs. Adam)
421 Cambridge Way   C: (818) 825-3469
Bolingbrook, IL 60440-1145   Birthday: Sept. 19
armysorella@yahoo.com   Admitted: July 7, 2003
Frederick Garst, PA, Pvt; John Rauch, PA, PS;
John Nicholas Garst, PA, PS; John Porter, NY, Pvt;
David Williams, CT, Pvt ; David Sage, CT, CS

968533 Lang, Allyson Noelle
4335 N. Kenmore 2nd Floor   H: (773) 771-7576
Chicago, IL 60613   Birthday: June 17
allyson.n.lang@gmail.com   Admitted: May 5, 2017
Bickford Lang, NH, PS

557354 Larson, Christine Arnesen (Mrs. James)
10245 Tybow Trl.   H: (815) 623-7940
Roscoe, IL 61073-8511   Birthday: June 27
Admitted: Feb. 1, 1971
Adam Deininger, PA, Pvt ; Christopher Stophel Earnest, PA, Pvt;
Abraham Liter, MD, PS ; Henry Nagle, PA, Sgt ;
Martin Riser, VA, Sol PS ; Christian Seltzer, PA, Pvt PS

952173 Lavery, Shannon Margaret*
310 S. Michigan Ave. Unit 802   H: (304) 690-0360
Chicago, IL 60604-4226   Birthday: June 12
laverysm@gmail.com   Admitted: Dec. 5, 2015
Oliver Bartlett, MA, Noncom

956308 Levin, Diane Scarpa*
1000 W. Washington Blvd. Unit 326   H: (609) 432-3465
Chicago, IL 60607-2153   Birthday: Nov. 15
diane.scarpa@ubs.com   Admitted: April 5, 2016
Daniel Chatfield, CT, Capt

986474 Lindsay, Andris Schroetter*
1432 Bonnie Brae Pl.
River Forest, IL 60305-1202
andrislindsay@gmail.com
David Bryant, NJ, Pvt

H: (708) 860-0911
Birthday: Sept. 11
Admitted: Nov. 5, 2018

986473 Lindsay, Bryant Schroetter*
1432 Bonnie Brae Pl.
River Forest, IL 60305-1202
15blindsay@gmail.com
David Bryant, NJ, Pvt

H: (708) 828-7617
Birthday: Nov. 16
Admitted: Nov. 5, 2018

933291 Louderman, Iris Chrisse Knight (Mrs. James Edward)
2605 S. Indiana Ave. Unit 2406
Chicago, IL 60616-2880
ilouderman@comcast.net
John Beard, SC, Pvt

C: 312-636-6639
Birthday: April 19
Admitted: June 5, 2014

828937 Lundin, Cheri Wynne
405 N. Wabash Ave Unit 911
Chicago, IL 60611-7658
clundin1620@gmail.com
Abraham Livermore, MA, Pvt CS

H: (312) 222-1514
Birthday: Oct.12
Admitted: July 5, 2004

871982 Lyshkow, Mary Ann Sippel (Mrs. Norman Arthur)
3550 N. Lake Shore Dr. Apt. 2702
Chicago, IL 60657-1913
mlsippel@aol.com
Abraham J Van Alstyne, NY, Col

H: (773) 935-1806
Birthday: May 27
Admitted: April 25, 2009

846012 MacLaren, Anne Louise
3753 N. Narragansett Ave.
Chicago, IL 60634-2427
almaclaren@sbcglobal.net
Joseph Rockwell, Jr, CT, Pvt

C: (773) 576-5085
Birthday: Aug. 29
Admitted: Oct. 7, 2006

962531 Magnus, Kristin Renee Wawzysko (Mrs. Jason Eric)
134 Chapel Hill Dr.
Battle Creek, MI 49015-4632
kris11403@yahoo.com
Simeon Raymond, CT, PS

H: (269) 580-7776
Birthday: Jan. 21
Admitted: 5 Oct. 5, 2016

878227　Malloy, Catherine Mary
6007 N. Sheridan Rd. Apt. 22J　　H: (773) 507-3884
Chicago, IL 60660-3064　　　　　Birthday: Jan. 22
malloy.malloy13@gmail.com　　　Admitted: Dec. 12, 2009
James Jones, NC, Capt PS

816086　Marshall, Lydia B. Heenan
1349 Lexington Ave Apt 2C　　　H: (212) 879-2176
New York, NY 10128-1514　　　　Birthday: Feb. 4
lbheenan@aol.com　　　　　　　Admitted: Feb. 1, 2003
Isaac Baldwin, CT, Sol

843700　Martinez, Traci Lynn ✪
4148 N. Avers Ave. Apt. 2D　　H: (773) 510-0751
Chicago, IL 60618-1904　　　　Birthday: June 8
tmartinez.dar@comcast.net　　Admitted: June 26, 2006
Levi Brown, MA, Capt

997588　McCaughey, Eleanor
3936 W. Eddy St.　　　　　　Birthday: 30 Jun
Chicago, IL 60618-5016　　　Admitted: August 5, 2019
John Banning; DE; CS, PS, Pvt

986140　McClure, Kathleen Jeanette (Mrs. Michael Jack)
5869 N. Kilbourn Ave.　　　H: (773) 777-6731
Chicago, IL 60646-5937　　Birthday: March 23
kmcclure323@yahoo.com　Admitted: Nov. 5, 2018
Levi Forbes, CT, Pvt

692847　McCoy, Ruth Sherrod (Mrs. Euell E)
830 Audubon Way HG415　　H: 847-383-5915
Lincolnshire, IL 60092　　　Birthday: June 15
mccoyrs@gmail.com　　　　Admitted: June 11, 1985
Oliver Alexander, VA, Sol CS; John Bolton, MD, PS;
Robert Bolton, GA, Pvt

991015　McKelvie, Linda Lea
7007 Chestnut Hill St.　　　　　　Birthday: Jan. 25
Highlands Ranch, CO 80130-5112 Admitted: March 5, 2019
Davemckelvie@comcast.net
Andrew Shearer, MD & PA, Cpl PS

986482 McKelvie, Shannon Ashlea*
3200 Westminster Ave.
Dallas, TX 75205-1427
samckelvie1@gmail.com
Andrew Shearer, MD & PA, Cpl PS

H: (303) 906-5858
Birthday: May 17
Admitted: Nov. 5, 2018

992843 Mearsheimer, Julia Webb*
1345 E. Park Pl.
Chicago, IL 60637-1767
j.mearsh@gmail.com
Michael Heisley, PA, Pvt PS

H: (773) 573-2076
Birthday: Sept.15
Admitted: April 5, 2019

986485 Mearsheimer, Pamela Trumbull Webb (Mrs. John Joseph)
1345 E. Park Pl.
Chicago, IL 60637-1767
pmearsh@gmail.com
Michael Heisley, PA, Pvt PS

H: (773) 551-1455
Birthday: July 25
Admitted: Nov. 5, 2018

990351 Mellon, Rebecca Jane Delco (Mrs. Michael Edward)
6225 N. Melvina Ave.
Chicago, IL 60646-3718
Michaelbeckyian@comcast.net
Phillip Austin, NY & MA, Pvt

H: (773) 774-5892
Birthday: Sept. 23
Admitted: Feb. 5, 2019

873339 Mihalas, Alexandra Genevieve
130 S. Canal St. Apt. 604
Chicago, IL 60606-3909
alexandra.mihalas@gmail.com
David Bemis, MA, Pvt

H: (312) 715-0744
Birthday: Aug. 9
Admitted: July 6, 2009

986141 Miller, Andrea Kristin*
1560 N. Sandburg Ter. Apt. 404J
Chicago, IL 60610-7702
andrea.miller34@gmail.com
Levi Forbes, CT, Pvt

H: (773) 401-6923
Birthday: Dec. 28
Admitted: Nov. 5, 2018

986142 Miller, Teresa Danielle*
2238 W. Wilson Ave.
Chicago, IL 60625-2125
miller.teresa98@gmail.com
Levi Forbes, CT, Pvt

H: (773) 401-6943
Birthday: May 19
Admitted: Nov. 5, 2018

957246 **Milton, Kristin Ann**
2859 N. Burling St. # 3C
Chicago, IL 60657-5215   Birthday: March 22
kristinmilton@aol.com   Admitted: May 5, 2016
Elias Teeter, PA, Pvt

973150 **Minnich, Valerie Joan***
707 W. Wellington Ave. Apt. 2   H: (773) 747-0522
Chicago, IL 60657-5337   Birthday: Sept. 18
valjmin@gmail.com   Admitted: Sept. 5, 2017
William Hildreth, CT, Pvt

645109 **Missimer, Elizabeth Katharine Doty (Mrs. Lyman, III)**
2520 Robinhood St. Apt. 1400   H: (936) 499-8698
Houston, TX 77005-2560   Birthday: June 30
betsymissimer@gmail.com   Admitted: April 16, 1980
Aaron Wright, PA, 2Lt

940094 **Molina, Deborah Kay Gillespie (Mrs. Oscar Edgardo)**
1845 W. Erie St.   H: (312) 243-4801
Chicago, IL 60622-5520   Birthday: Nov. 3
dmolina113@hotmail.com   Admitted: Feb. 5, 2015
George Gillespie, VA, PS

995817 **Morgese, Mary Grace ***
535 N. Michigan Ave. Apt. 3111   H: (630) 200-0011
Chicago, IL 60611-3866   Birthday: June 4
Marygrace.morgese@gmail.com   Admitted: July 5, 2019
William Edmands, PA, PS

820890 **Morony, Mary Patricia**
1660 N. La Salle Dr. Apt. 2808   H: (312) 944-7029
Chicago, IL 60614-6021   Birthday: July 25
mmorony@ameritech.net   Admitted: July 13, 2003
Levi Adams, NH, Sgt

973319 **Morris, Caitlin Elisabeth***
161 W. Kinzie St. Apt. 1210   H: (317) 777-0726
Chicago, IL 60654-4737   Birthday: Aug. 12
CaitElis@gmail.com   Admitted: Sept. 5, 2017
Isaac Townsend, PA, Pvt

904384 **Morrissy, Anne Elizabeth**
3270 N. Lake Shore Dr. Apt. 7C   H: (262) 745-4001
Chicago, IL 60657-3917   Birthday: June 25
morrissya@gmail.com   Admitted: April 21, 2012
James Huntley, CT, Capt

942240 **Moss, Gail Carol Sutliff (Mrs. Joseph)**
2450 N. Lakeview Ave. # 3A   H: (312) 933-0562
Chicago, IL 60614-2878   Birthday: Dec. 25
gailcmoss@gmail.com   Admitted: April 5, 2015
Abel Sutliff, CT, Pvt

895118 **Moylan, Eileen Marie Hoganson (Mrs. Martin F.)**
1614 S. Charlotte Ct.   H: (630) 638-3589
Lombard, IL 60148-6148   Birthday: March 11
eileenhmoylan@gmail.com   Admitted: June 27, 2011
John Van Bibber, VA, Capt

562357 **Nagel, Margaret Elizabeth Sowa (Mrs. Walter)**
175 E. Delaware Pl. Apt. 6709   C: (312) 301-6400
Chicago, IL 60611-7733   Birthday: Nov. 3
meggnagel@aol.com   Admitted: Oct. 16, 1971
William Moore, NC & VA, Pvt

770508 **Nelson, Sonja Elizabeth**
1540 W. Chase Ave. Apt. 3W
Chicago, IL 60626-2154   Birthday: April 20
snelsonchi@gmail.com   Admitted: April 1996
James Sappington, PA, Pvt

958100 **Neilitz, Stephanie Marie***
625 Brummel St. Apt. 1   H: (218) 329-7499
Evanston, IL 60202-5216   Birthday: Nov. 13
stephanieneilitz.dar@gmail.com   Admitted: June 5, 2016
Samuel Hayes, NH, Capt PS; Lemuel Bishop, VT, Sgt

82665 **Nesti, Mary Alice**
2400 N. Lakeview Ave. Apt. 506   H: (773) 248-8943
Chicago, IL 60614-2732   Birthday: Dec 23
maryalice506@icloud.com   Admitted: Oct. 18, 1961
Joshua Dewees, DE, Pvt; Jonas Ward, MA, Sgt

956721 Neumann, Katherine Joan*
2917 N. Melvina Ave.   H: (773) 318-3501
Chicago, IL 60634-5006   Birthday: May 11
ktneumann@live.com   Admitted: May 5, 2016
Robert Galbraith, PA, Pvt

956720 Neumann-Bacastow, Karen Michelle*
2900 N. Mango Ave.   H: (773) 848-4347
Chicago, IL 60634-5237   Birthday: May 16
kneumann1988@gmail.com   Admitted: May 5, 2016
Robert Galbraith, PA, Pvt

988396 Nicolini, Palesa Anne Jackson (Mrs. Allan Daniel Rios)
4635 Mira Loma St.   H: (773) 895-6598
Castro Valley, CA 94546-2313   Birthday: March 7
palesajnicolini@gmail.com   Admitted: Jan. 5, 2019
Edward Haymond, VA & PA, Pvt

840870 Nowlin, Janet Lynn
2768 N. Buffalo Grove Rd. Apt. 308 H: (773) 343-4237
Arlington Heights, IL 60004-7324   Birthday: Sept. 7
JanetLNowlin@gmail.com   Admitted: Feb. 4, 2006
Christian Sockman, PA, Pvt

986516 O'Brien, Emily Dey (Mrs. Gannon Patrick)*
811 W. 15th Pl. Unit 503   H: (973) 818-0486
Chicago, IL 60608-1641   Birthday: Sept. 16
emily.dey916@gmail.com   Admitted: Nov. 5, 2018
George Stansill, NY, Pvt

835776 Ohlrich, Keri Lynn Schoenborn (Mrs. Stephen Paul)
1747 Oakwood St.   H: (414) 763-7919
Pasadena, CA 91104-1511   Birthday: Sept. 30
keri_orlrich@hotmail.com   Admitted: July 5, 2005
Christian Eby, PA, Pvt

641189 Osgood, Winifred Lee
2033 Butterfly Ln. Apt. CC407   H: (630) 717-8991
Naperville, IL 60563-5313   Birthday: Feb.16
lee_osgood@yahoo.com   Admitted: Oct. 13, 1979
William Osgood, MA, Pvt

547779 **Ostfeld, Lynne Ruthann**
300 N. State St. Apt. 5405   H: (312) 467-5692
Chicago, IL 60654-5470   Birthday: Dec. 1
lynnepersonal@rcn.com   Admitted: Jan. 31,1970
Andrew Bailey, NH, Cpl PS; David Collins, PA, Pvt;
Ephraim Gilmore, PA, Pvt PS; Gershom Twitchell, Sr, NH, PS

886200 **Padgett, Amy Elizabeth (Mrs. Greeley Stivers)**
11134 Carrington Green Dr.   H: (571) 212-5397
Glen Allen, VA 23060-3446   Birthday: Sept. 24
amypadgettkoch@gmail.com   Admitted: Oct. 9, 2010
Joseph Williams, Jr, NC, Lt

938556 **Pancero, Katheryn Lynn**
1446 N. Dearborn 2B   C: (773) 573-7307
Chicago, IL 60610   Birthday: Sept 4
dzlildemon@gmail.com   Admitted: Dec. 5, 2014
Samuel Fenton, PA, Capt

928982 **Pawlak Jamie Krukewitt**
5368 N. Lowell Ave.   H: (773) 520- 0792
Chicago, IL 60630-1736   Birthday: July 18
jamie.pawlak@astellas.com   Admitted: Feb. 5, 2014
Floyd Abraham, SC,Pvt

882418 **Peirce, Ellen Maureen (Mrs. Roger Michael Dore)**
5774 N. Caldwell Ave.   H: (773) 205-7147
Chicago, IL 60646-6648   Birthday: July 26
empeirce1@yahoo.com   Admitted: July 5, 2010
Joseph Spalding, CT, Ens

771156 **Perry, Barbara Burditt (Mrs. Michael Richard)**
326 Prospect Ave.   H: (630) 858-8393
Glen Ellyn, IL 60137-4914   Birthday: July 22
Admitted: April 13, 1996
Samuel Burdett, MA, 2Lt

886617   Perry, Laura Amanda
1738 W. Erie St.   H: (773) 929-3486
Chicago, IL 60622-6017   Birthday: Feb. 28
amandaperry@gmail.com   Admitted: Oct. 9, 2010
Thomas Paine, Jr, VA, Pvt

875666   Peterson, Sharon Beth Rich (Mrs. Charles Irving)
5226 N. Sawyer Ave.   H: (773) 218-8281
Chicago, IL 60625-4716   Birthday: Feb.11
speterson@igc.org   Admitted: Oct. 3, 2009
Ephraim Wilson, MA, Pvt PS

955956   Pettyjohn, Kara Megan
630B N. Ashland Ave. Apt. B3E   H: (617) 680-2626
Chicago, IL 60640-4642   Birthday: Aug. 4
kara.pettyjohn@gmail.com   Admitted: April 5, 2016
Joseph Stevens, NY, Cpl

992834   Pool, Bonnie Jean
1555 N. Sandburg Terr. Apt. 516   H: (312) 664-2123
Chicago, IL 60610-6323   Birthday: May 12
bpool@rcn.com   Admitted: April 5, 2019
David Baldwin, NJ, Pvt

909421   Post, Ashley Elizabeth Trent (Mrs. Jacob August)*
324 Brandon Ave.   Birthday: June 19
Glen Ellyn, IL 60137-4902   Admitted: Oct. 6, 2012
ashley.elizabeth.post@gmail.com
Ephraim Tucker, NJ, PS

555491   Pratt, Linda Sue
2052 N. Lincoln Park W. Apt. 1510 H: (312) 771-4952
Chicago, IL 60614-4745   Birthday: Oct. 5
lprattbethany@yahoo.com   Admitted: Dec. 10, 1970
Benedict Burlingame, Jr, RI, Pvt

973960   Pritzker, Mary Kathryn Muenster
1435 N. Astor St.   H: (312) 560-1114
Chicago, IL 60610-3099   Birthday: May 25
MKP@evergreenfarm.net   Admitted: Oct. 5, 2017
Benjamin Goble, PA, Pvt

892418 Pryor, Kelli Ann Watts (Mrs. Blakely Justin)
6116 Persimmon Ct.   Birthday: March 5
Kansas City, MO 64152-3140   Admitted: April 9, 2011
kelliann@kc.rr.com
Alexander Crockett, VA, Sol

962196 Ramento, Corie Ann Walcott (Mrs. Adam Elika)*
1833 W. Erie St. # 1   H: (508) 380-0055
Chicago, IL 60622-5520   Birthday: Feb. 12
coriewalcott@gmail.com   Admitted: Oct. 5, 2016
George Walcott, RI, Pvt

924514 Reddan, Damaris Welcker (Mrs. John Michael)
1235 W. George St. Apt.103   Birthday: Aug. 6
Chicago, IL 60657-4815   Admitted: Oct. 5, 2013
rissa.reddan@us.pwc.com
Roger Fuller, CT, PS

Kristen J. Richardson
5442 S. Cornell Ave. Apt. 2S   H: (312) 420-4836
Chicago, IL 60615-5675
kristen.judithr@gmail.com

968059 Ridgeway, Lydia Pearl*
5000 N. Keeler Ave.   H: (312) 420-4836
Chicago, IL 60630-2716   Birthday: March 14
lydiaridgeway@gmail.com   Admitted: April 5, 2017
Samuel Ridgeway, SC, Pvt

900061 Ridgeway, Rachel Elise*
1000 W. 15th St. Unit 114   H: (773) 736-5672
Chicago, IL 60608-1438   Birthday: March 1
reridgeway@gmail.com   Admitted: Dec. 10, 2011
Samuel Ridgeway, SC, Pvt

942264 Robinett, Rhonda Kaye Bartlett
2727 N. Mont Clare Ave.   H: (773) 206-2726
Chicago, IL 60707-1608   Birthday: Oct. 25
rhondarobinett@gmail.com   Admitted: April 5, 2015
Jeremiah Dial, SC, Pvt.; William Woodward, GA, PS

959758 Roll, Lydia Shanklin
5316 S. Dorchester Ave. Apt. 416   H: (812) 318-7070
Chicago, IL 60615-5366   Birthday: Nov. 29
lydiaroll@gmail.com   Admitted: Aug.5, 2016
George Poage, VA, Col PS; Matthias Roll, NJ, Pvt;
Patrick Sharkey, VA, PS

993773 Rolley, Larissa Renee
621 S. Plymouth Ct. Apt. 701   H: (312) 282-9965
Chicago, IL 60605-1856   Birthday: Sept.11
larissarr@hotmail.com   Admitted: May 5, 2019
Littleton Chandler, VA, Pvt

989451 Roy, Ellora Hamilton
568 Golfview Dr.   H: (630) 244-5754
Barrington, IL 60010-2045   Birthday: May 29
roye@cooley.edu   Admitted: Feb.5, 2019
William Hamilton, NJ, Sol

889798 Roy, Penny Sue Lindert (Mrs. BiJay Kumar)
1175 Woodburn Ct.   H: (847) 744-0100
Inverness, IL 60067-4290   Birthday: Aug. 9,
pennylroy@aol.com   Admitted: Feb. 5, 2011
William Hamilton, NJ, Sol

956860 Saint George, Marlene Marie Sanguinett (Mrs. Gerald William)
210 E. Pearson St. Apt. 3A   H: (312) 953-1617
Chicago, IL 60611-7336   Birthday: Oct. 21
mssstgeorge@aol.com   Admitted: May 5, 2016
John Skidmore, VA, Maj CS

896398 Sandburg, Eileen Elizabeth Bailey (Mrs. Mark David)
130 S. Canal St. Apt. 615   H: (936) 525-9446
Chicago, IL 60606-3909   Birthday: Sept. 11
Elohrengel@aol.com   Admitted: Oct. 8, 2011
Matthew Newton, CT, CS PS

925510 **Sapio, Lori Kathleen**
2728 W. Polk St.
Chicago, IL 60612-4034
sapiosis@yahoo.com
Abdiel Mcclure, PA, Lt PS

H: (312) 972-3483
Birthday: April 4
Admitted: Dec.7, 2013

965291 **Schick, Alexandra Elizabeth***
2048 N. Cleveland Ave. Apt.212
Chicago, IL 60614
alexa@conlonrealestate.com
Nathan Adams, CT, Lt

H: (312) 515-7191
Birthday: Aug 8
Admitted: Jan. 5, 2017

517948 **Schickner, Ann**
25 West Randolph #2906
Chicago, Il 60601-3526
acschickn@yahoo. com
Thomas Woods, PA, Pvt ; Charles Canary, PA, Pvt;
Thomas Cracroft, VA, PS ; Isaac Dawson, VA, PS;
Rowland Alexander, NC, Lt PS

H: (217) 414-9102
Birthday: Oct. 10
Admitted: Oct.15, 1966

937338 **Seewald, Natalie Marie***
3139 S. Emerald Ave. Apt. 2R
Chicago, IL 60616-5263
natalieseewald@gmail.com
David Beckwith, MA, Cpl

H: (630) 362-3251
Birthday: May 1
Admitted: Nov. 5, 2014

971177 **Sharp, Elizabeth Gleason Dillon (Mrs. Jeffrey Smith)**
222 E. Chestnut St. Apt. 3B
Chicago, IL 60611-2306
lsharp@sharp-law.com
Alexander Peden, SC, Pvt

H: (312) 346-1726
Birthday: Feb. 19
Admitted: July 5, 2017

964399 **Shelley, Sandra White (Mrs. Colbert)**
13405 Central Park Ave.
Robbins, IL 60472-1105
saundrashelley@sbcglobal.net
Veteran, Navy Josiah Milton, VA, PS

H: (708) 642-4976
Birthday: Feb. 28
Admitted: Dec. 5, 2016

472067   Shields, Andree Keane
1212 N. Lake Shore Dr. Apt. 22CN   C: (630) 209-7300
Chicago, IL 60610-6680   Birthday: Oct. 15
andrees@rcn.com   Admitted: Feb. 1, 1960
John Goddard, Sr, MA, CS PS

989242   Shrum, Brittanie Skye
1720 S. Michigan Ave.   H: (312) 216-9777
Chicago, IL 60616-1465   Birthday: Sept.14
skyeshrum@yahoo.com   Admitted: Feb. 5, 2019
Seth Thompson, NC, Sol

875469   Simons, Joyce Evelyn Salsbury (Mrs. Marvin)
3850 Lampson Ave. # 127   H: (626) 264-0493
Sunrise Assisted Living   Birthday: Feb. 17
Seal Beach, CA 90740-2797   Admitted: Oct. 3, 2009
stking@rcn.com
Joseph Palmer, CT, Capt

885129   Skurek, Heather Ashley Green
4510 Sussex Dr.   H: (412) 559-2192
Columbus, OH 43220-3860   Birthday: March 7
hegreen@gmail.com   Admitted: Oct. 9, 2010
Andrew Finley, PA, Lt

492859   Slovacek, Charmaine
17925 Cynthia Dr.   H: (612) 470-0594
Minnetonka, MN 55345-4204   Birthday: Oct. 24
Admitted: 1 Feb 1963
Edmund Pillsbury, NH, Pvt

848326   Smart, Becky Sue Stecher (Mrs. Hugh Frederick)
2806 N. Oakley Ave. Apt. 303   H: (847) 302-2994
Chicago, IL 60618-8060   Birthday: Aug. 7
Becky.smart.dar@gmail.com   Admitted: Feb. 3 2007
Andrew Appell, PA, PS; John Mitchell, PA, Pvt;
Andrew Shearer, MD & PA, Cpl PS

989298 Smith, Jane Ellen
3936 W. Eddy St.
Chicago, IL 60618-5016
janeandpat@sbcglobal.net
John Banning, DE, Pvt CS PS

H: (773) 719-6151
Birthday: Nov.13
Admitted: Feb. 5, 2019

883263 Smith, Rachael Katharine Hoffman*
1635 W. Rosehill Dr.
Chicago, IL 60660-4017
suzhof11@gmail.com
Peter Cartwright, VA, Sol

H: (202) 352-0508
Birthday: Oct. 8

955114 Snorf, Margaret
55 W. Delaware Pl. Apt. 512
Chicago, IL 60610-3388
peggysnorf@aol.com
Henry Warner, PA, Pvt ; John Dickerman, VT, Pvt

H: (312) 787-9746
Birthday: May 15
Admitted: Mar. 5, 2016

929511 Sokolow, Raychelle Betty Logan (Mrs. Daniel Alan)
812 Viewpointe Dr.
Saint Charles, IL 60174-4183
dsokolow9@gmail.com
Benjamin Ring, PA, Pvt PS

H: (707) 489-1137
Birthday: Aug. 25
Admitted: March 5, 2014

928556 Stanley, Jordan Lynne*
9407 Smoke Hollow Rd.
Kernersville, NC 27284-9079
stanleyjo12@students.ecu.edu
Thomas Paine, Jr, VA, Pvt

H: (336) 423-7848
Birthday: Feb. 17
Admitted: Feb. 5, 2014

922031 Stanley, Melissa Coxe
3804 W. Wrightwood Ave.
Chicago, IL 60647-1033
mstan99@aol.com
Joseph Slate, MA, Capt CS PS

Birthday: Dec. 17
Admitted: Oct. 5, 2013

962222 Stanton, Maria Johanna Keller (Mrs. John Thomas)
900 S. Clark St. Apt. 1802
Chicago, IL 60605-3696
mariajstanton@gmail.com
Henson Johnson, VA, Pvt

H: (206) 334-8772
Birthday: Feb. 9
Admitted: Oct. 5, 2016

959761 Stapleton-Corcoran, Erin Louise (Mrs. Steven John)
2546 W. Cortland St.   H: (773) 960-6070
Chicago, IL 60647-4308   Birthday: Dec. 13
estaple@gmail.com   Admitted: Aug. 5, 2016
John Cundiff, VA, Noncom

981911 Starr, Kathryn Leann
1833 Wildberry Drive A   H: (248) 961-6116
Glenview, IL 60025   Birthday: August 14
starr9003@yahoo.com   Admitted: May 5, 2018
John Loughridge

980591 Startz, Elizabeth Anne Kelliher-Paz (Mrs. William McNamara)*
1923 N. Richmond St. Apt. 1   H: (708) 207-7411
Chicago, IL 60647-3936   Birthday: May 31
elizabeth.a.startz@gmail.com   Admitted: May 5, 2018
Enoch Hayden, MA, Sgt

Sarah Elizabeth Stearns
301 Governors Drive   (630) 670-7272
Hendersonville, NC 28791
Sarah.librarydirector@gmail.com

982726 Stephens, Myra Frances Tidwell (Mrs. Bradford Taylor)
2111 W. Churchill St. Apt. 213   H: (904) 887-7178
Chicago, IL 60647-5577   Birthday: March 20
myrastephens@gmail.com   Admitted: July 5, 2018
John Walden, VA, Pvt

871970 Stewart, Nancy Virginia Hankins (Mrs. Jeremy Wayne)
P.O. Box 241962   H: (662) 801-0040
Omaha, NE 68124-6962   Birthday: April 1
nancyhankins@hotmail.com   Admitted: April 25, 2009
Moses Dalton, VA, Sgt

857330 Stivers, Madeline Wortham*
1874 N. Halsted St. Apt. 2W   H: (812) 202-0827
Chicago, IL 60614-6456   Birthday: Sept 16
Admitted: Dec. 8, 2007
James Hunt, MD, Pvt

995862 **Stott, Christine McKee Anderson (Mrs. Bradley Colin)**
4113 Linder Pl. H: (630) 272-0000
Rockford, IL 61107-1434 Birthday: March 3
christystott@gmail.com Admitted: July 5, 2019
Thomas Odell, MD, Lt

997599 **Sturhahn, Jennifer**
332 S. Santa Anita Ave.
Pasadena, CA 91107-5275 (202) 906-9291
jackson@gps.caltech.edu Birthday: April 4
Edward Haymond, VA, Pvt Admitted: August 5, 2019

969941 **Sullens, Stephanie Rebecca**
5400 W. Sienna Ln. Apt. 2104 H: (573) 823-4668
Peoria, IL 61615-7856 Birthday: Nov. 5
stephaniersullens@gmail.com Admitted: June 5, 2017
William Hough, VA, Noncom

607198 **Sumner, Sara**
1617 N. Hoyne Ave. H: (773) 276-1060
Chicago, IL 60647-5408 Birthday: June 2
sum1934@aol.com Admitted: April 17, 1976
Dominick Egle, PA, Pvt

843843 **Sutton Brieva, Jennifer Ann**
2052 N. Lincoln Park W. Apt. 901 C: (312) 560-9974
Chicago, IL 60614-4743 Birthday: April 3
jsuttonbrieva@gmail.com Admitted: June 26, 2006
John Adam Walrath, NY, Pvt

965631 **Swafford, Nichole Leighann***
5910 N. Sheridan Rd. Apt. 201 C: (312) 929-5391
Chicago, IL 60660-5103 Birthday: Aug. 8
nichole.swafford@gmail.com Admitted: Feb. 5, 2017
Richard Wright, Sr, NC, PS

980938 **Tarrson, Linda Christopher (Mrs. Emanuel B.)**
1040 N. Lake Shore Dr. Apt. 9A H: (312) 498-1934
Chicago, IL 60611-1105 Birthday: Feb. 5
ltarrson@aol.com Admitted: May 5, 2018
Moses Evans, NJ, PS

889747 Tausche', Louise Gaylord Ingersoll (Mrs. Thomas John)
1448 N. Lake Shore Dr. Apt. 9B   H: (312) 787-3806
Chicago, IL 60610-1799   Birthday: March 8
LITmails@aol.com   Admitted: Feb. 5 2011
Cornelius Wynkoop Swartwout, NY, Pvt

880024 Taylor, Wendy Ann Lohr (Mrs. Joseph Paul)
5510 N. Sheridan Rd. Apt. 14A   C: (773) 495-3390
Chicago, IL 60640-1630   Birthday: Aug. 7
taylohr@gmail.com   Admitted: Feb. 6, 2010
John Hereford, Sr, VA, PS

892423 Temple, Margaret Ann
1759 N. Cleveland Ave.   H: (312) 943-0362
Chicago, IL 60614-5602   Birthday: June 10
temple.a12@gmail.com   Admitted: April 9, 2011
Alexander Turrentine, NC, CS PS

891103 Thomas, Suzanne Jeanne
4419 N. Francisco Ave.   H: (773) 588-6874
Chicago, IL 60625-3806   Birthday: Aug. 29
sthomas4419@gmail.com   Admitted: April 9, 2011
John Gebhart, MD, Noncom

961338 Tossi, Susan Lorraine Welter (Mrs. Barry Allen)
420 E. Ohio St Apt 21E   H: (608) 792-1776
Chicago, IL 60611-4657   Birthday: Sept. 7
swtossi@yahoo.com   Admitted: Sept. 5, 2016
Oliver Powers, MA, Pvt

973458 Towey, Emma Catherine Harris (Mrs. Evan Barlett)*
3881 Yellowstone Way SW   H: (770) 979-5742
Lilburn, GA 30047-2585   Birthday: Sept. 21
eh01386@icloud.com   Admitted: Oct. 5, 2017
George Van Der Veer, VA, Pvt

959862 Ungaretti, Noren Gail Woody (Mrs. Richard Anthony)
740 W. Willow St.   H: (312) 864-2304
Chicago, IL 60614-5151   Birthday: June 5
norenungaretti@yahoo.com   Admitted: Aug. 5, 2016
Rezin Beall, MD, BGen

920518   **Vanoye, Christi Anne Ray (Mrs. Carlos Guillermo)**
512 N. McClurg Ct. Apt. 2601
Chicago, IL 60611-4165   Birthday: Jan. 3
cvanoye@equinoxis.com   Admitted: June 24, 2013
Baylis Earle, SC, Pvt PS

875704   **Vasquez, Kathleen Anne Hickey (Mrs. Luis Felipe)**
3718 N. Newcastle Ave.   H: (773) 612-0079
Chicago, IL 60634-2350   Birthday: Aug. 6
kathy.vasquez@sbcglobal.net   Admitted: Oct. 3, 2009
Timothy Dustin, NH, PS

967405   **Veltrop, Gayle Leslie Suydam (Mrs. Loren)**
888 S. Michigan Ave. Unit 801   H: (847) 772-5832
Chicago, IL 60605-2249   Birthday: Jan. 30
gayle@veltrop.com   Admitted: April 5, 2017
John Suydam, NJ, Pvt

891105   **Villa, Jacqueline Nicole***
511 W. Division St. Apt. 406   H: (312) 758-5046
Chicago, IL 60610-1802   Birthday: July 22
jackievillaDAR@gmail.com   Admitted: April 9, 2011
William Crittenden Webb, VA, Sol PS

905372   **Waller, Sharon Ann (Mrs. David)**
4916 N. Francisco Ave.   H: (773) 878-1354
Chicago, IL 60625-3608   Birthday: Feb. 7
sharonwaller@u.northwestern.edu Admitted: April 21, 2012
Willis Murphy Watson, SC, Lt

880833   **Walsh, Deborah Ann Paschal (Mrs. Joseph Aloysius, Jr)**
55 W. Delaware Pl. Apt. 207   H: (312) 787-8984
Chicago, IL 60610-6087   Birthday: Nov. 20
deborahwalsh@sbcglobal.net   Admitted: April 17, 2010
John Fulkerson, NJ, Pvt

952174   **Walsh, Erin Kathryn***
1530 S. State St. Apt. 831   H: (304) 633-1260
Chicago, IL 60605-2984   Birthday: May 12
eklavery@gmail.com   Admitted: Dec. 5, 2015
Oliver Bartlett, MA, Noncom

962529 Wawzysko, Debra Lee Raymond (Mrs. Stanley Michael)
9100 Division Dr.   H: (269) 420-0078
Ceresco, MI 49033-9638   Birthday: April 17
debwawz@msn.com   Admitted: Oct. 5, 2016
Simeon Raymond, CT, PS

825157 Webb, Catherine Louise
2440 N. Lakeview Ave. # 12A   H: (773) 404-9040
Chicago, IL 60614-2872   Birthday: Sept. 7
cathywebbmd@gmail.com   Admitted: Feb. 7, 2004
George Wenner, PA, Noncom

961903 Weinberg, Diane Ruth Stilwell (Mrs. Richard)
180 E. Pearson St. Apt. 3906   H: (312) 952-7808
Chicago, IL 60611-6733   Birthday: Nov. 23
stilwelldiane@gmail.com
Benjamin Harrison, VA, Col

954899 Weinberger, Allison Elaine*
1360 N. Lake Shore Dr. Apt. 207   H: (847) 337-6595
Chicago, IL 60610-2149   Birthday: Jan. 9
alliweinberger@gmail.com   Admitted: March 5, 2016
Walter Dickinson, NJ, Pvt

891070 Welch, Ayten Williamson (Mrs. David Charles)
9 Gale Ave.   H: (217) 638-6389
River Forest, IL 60305-2009   Birthday: July 11
aytenai@aol.com   Admitted: April 9, 2011
Robert Kirkpatrick, SC, Pvt

886717 White, Karen Connie Hutson (Mrs. Ray R. White)
3200 N. Lake Shore Dr. Apt. 1505 H: (773) 549-6541
Chicago, IL 60657-3949   Birthday: Oct. 12
raywhiteassoc@att.net   Admitted: Oct. 9, 2010
Jacob Groat, VA, Pvt

832992 Wilcox, Pamela Peters Schoenborn (Mrs. Robert John)
10290 Stonegate Rd.   H: (773) 857-2391
Cedarburg, WI 53012-9567   Birthday: July 29
pjwilcox@rcn.com   Admitted: Feb 5, 2005
Christian Eby, PA, Pvt

968032 **Wilson, Jeanneen Alexsandra Holmes**
(Mrs. Kenneth Mashawn)
13405 Central Park Ave.   H: (708) 915-0448
Robbins, IL 60472-1105   Birthday: Sept. 6
ybnvs9@gmail.com   Admitted: April 5, 2017
Josiah Milton, VA, PS

991062 **Witt, Mary Hillers**
130 E. Oak St.   H: (312) 428-6039
Chicago, IL 60611-1389   Birthday: Feb.1
WittMH@hotmail.com   Admitted: March 5, 2019
Caleb Abbott, MA, Sgt

909375 **Witzburg, Deborah Erin**
1658 N. Leavitt St.   Birthday: May 16
Chicago, IL 60647-5410   Admitted: Oct. 6 2012
deborah.witzburg@alumni.brown.edu
John Christy, NJ, Pvt

698313 **Wonderling, Ainsley Brook (Mrs. Robert)**
41413 N. Suraya Dr.   H: (847) 354-5637
Antioch, IL 60002-2176   Birthday: Nov. 24
ainsleywonderling@yahoo.com   Admitted: Feb 7, 1986
Christopher Keller, PA, Capt

942455 **Wood, Courtenay Robinson**
3306 Hartzell St.   C: 312-961-9816, H: 847-869-5822
Evanston, IL 60201-1130   Birthday: March 22
crwoodhnj@aol.com   Admitted: Apr. 5, 2015
George Shepard, VA, Pvt; Francis Mcdermot, Sr, VA, PS;
William Cloud, VA, PS; Richard Dickens, VA, Lt PS;
Henry Cloud, VA, PS; Henry Lewis, Jr, VA, Sol PS;
Henry Lewis, Sr, VA, PS

966890 **Wood, Jennifer Lynn**
2600 W. Winnemac Ave. Apt. 1B   H: (773) 562-3206
Chicago, IL 60625-2759   Birthday: June 17
chicagojenna@gmail.com   Admitted: March 5, 2017
Alexander Wood, VA, Pvt

925145 **Worzalla, Krista Ann***
121 W. Chestnut St. Apt. 1808   H: (414) 861-9034
Chicago, IL 60610-3161   Birthday: June 8
krista.worzalla@gmail.com   Admitted: Oct. 5, 2013
Moses Webster, CT, Pvt

865313 **Zingery, Sharon Kaye**
6157 N. Sheridan Rd. Apt. 25E   H: (773) 262-7699
Chicago, IL 60660-2827   Birthday: Oct. 23
szingery@gmail.com   Admitted: Oct. 4, 2008
Adam Miser, PA, Pvt ; George Mumma, PA, PS

853442 **Zukas, Mary Elizabeth Pabich**
14446 Vane St.
Bennington, NE 68007-1568   Birthday: Oct. 4
mzkola@cox.net   Admitted: June 25, 2007
Thomas Hartley, VA, PS

ASSOCIATE MEMBERS

817379   **Baumgarten, Marion Tucker Betor (Mrs. Jonathan David)**
106 S. Ridgeland Ave. Apt. 314   C: (708) 369-5488
Oak Park, IL 60302-4617   Admitted: April 12, 2003
marionbaumgarten41@gmail.com
Thomas Owsley, Sr, VA, PS; Joseph Bledsoe, VA, PS ;
Nicholas Trosper, NC, Capt; William Swift, NC,CS PS

895505   **Bell, Lorraine Diane (Mrs. Mark Weisdorf)**
959 1st Ave. Apt. 20C   C: (323) 681-4979
New York, NY 10022-6559   Admitted: July 3, 2011
lorraine@knickerbockerdar.org
Gideon Shepard, MA, Lt

970417   **Benson, Christine Marie Quigley (Mrs. Rex Edward)**
2235 Delaney Ave   H: (815) 434-0705
Ottawa, IL 61350-1280   Admitted: June 5, 2017
chris.benson52@gmail.com
Benjamin Harrison, VA, Col

701430   **Burt-Willson, Margaret Kay**
333 Rivard Blvd.   H: (313) 499-1689
Grosse Pointe, MI 48230-1625   Admitted: June 6, 1986
suite2006@live.com
Stephen Thompson, Sr, CT, Pvt CS PS

677742   **Craig, Roberta Elaine Deahl (Mrs. Charles William)**
5545 Via de Campo   H: (714) 692-8843
Yorba Linda, CA 92887-4916   Admitted: Oct. 14, 1983
recdar@roadrunner.com
Michael Conway, MD, Pvt PS

873597   **DeFrees, Janelle Dema Williamson**
(Mrs. David Lane (deceased))
4237 Lakeview Dr.   H: (913) 306-6279
Leavenworth, KS 66048-4929   Admitted: July 6, 2009
jdefrees@kc.rr.com
Peter Scholl, VA, Lt; Joseph Bryan, VA, PS;
Edward Boone, NC & VA, CS PS; Martha BRYAN Boone,
VA, PS; William Scholl, VA, PS; John Mundle, VA, Sgt;
James Mundle, PA, PS

927997 **Domain, Deborah Ann**
5749 N. Kerbs Ave.   H: (312) 787-1840
Chicago, IL 60646-6618   Admitted: Jan. 5, 2014
mydomain211@gmail.com
Joseph Copley, MA, Pvt; Noah Copley, MA, Pvt;
Samuel Snow, MA, Pvt; Lemuel Birdsall, NY, Pvt;
Joseph Kemp, MA, Pvt

955850 **Dugas, Kelly Ann**
738 Main St.   H: (857) 498-9332
Waltham, MA 02451-0616   Admitted: April 5, 2016
kellydugs272727@aol.com
Gideon Phillips, MA, Pvt

936731 **Graffius, Victoria Ann Warfield (Mrs. LeRoy Ralph)**
3225 Penbroke Pl   H: (859) 264-1070
Lexington, KY 40509-2015   Admitted: Oct. 5, 2014
vgraffius@equity-management.com
Seth Warfield, MD, PS

571850 **Gustafson, Mary Vandemore (Mrs. Glendon D)**
903 S. Spring St.   H: (309) 944-3115
Geneseo, IL 61254-1831   Admitted: Oct.13,1972
gustafson711@hotmail.com
John Harper, VA, CS PS ; Meredith Gainey, NC, PS;
Nehamiah Andrews, CT, PS ; Asa Andrews, CT, Pvt

693501 **Iseminger, Lois Elaine**
4300 N. Marine Dr. Apt. 1602   H: (773) 327-0281
Chicago, IL 60613-5802   Admitted: Oct. 11, 1985
lei4300@aol.com
Reuben Rugg, MA, Pvt ; Silas Allen, MA, Pvt;
Jonathan Hastings, MA, Sgt ; Daniel Rugg, MA, PS;
Benjamin Bacon, Jr, MA, Pvt CS ; Benjamin Bacon, Sr, MA, CS;
James Reed, MA, Pvt ; Stephen Moore, NJ, Pvt PS

863193 **Kovarik, Karen Dale Replogle**
158 Rushton Ln.   H: (305) 619-0237
Tavernier, FL 33070-3015   Admitted: July 7, 2008
karkovar6@gmail.com
Rinehart Replogle, Jr, PA, Pvt PS; Rinehart Replogle, Sr, PA, Pvt;
William Humphrey, RI, Maj PS; Daniel Tenney, MA, Pvt

532643 **Lee, Linda Lee Pennington (Mrs. Howard)**
30W345 Claymore Ln. H: (630) 983-9898
Naperville, IL 60563-1847 Admitted: April 13, 1968
howardlee3382@comcast.net
Henry Benn, Sr, DE, PS; Jacob Keller, PA, Sol;
Robert Pennington, MD, Pvt; James Watson, PA, PS

933125 **Lott, Karen Hamilton**
8215 159th Ave. H: (347) 599-6396
Howard Beach, NY 11414-2901 Admitted: June 5, 2014
karen.hamilton.lott@gmail.com
Zephaniah Lott, PA, Capt ; Henry Lott, PA, Capt

976816 **Marting, Sandra Jean Hensel (Mrs. Herbert)**
1290 Delaney Ferry Rd. H: (859) 296-0993
Nicholasville, KY 40356-8727 Admitted: Jan. 5, 2018
sandymartng@twc.com
Alexander Mack, PA, Pvt PS

645432 **Mattern, Christine (Mrs. Scott J)**
804 Winnie St. C: (281) 795-7635
Galveston, TX 77550-5131 Admitted: April 16, 1980
cginkens@comcast.net
Isaac Preston, Sr, NJ, Col

856584 **Mawhinney, Ida Diana Jones (Mrs. James I.)**
6233 N. Forest Glen Ave. C: (865) 806-8961
Chicago, IL 60646-5068 Admitted: Dec. 8, 2007
djm8736@gmail.com
Robert Sevier, NC, Capt

923429 **Meadows, Amy Laura**
3751 N. Lowell Ave. H: (312) 315-2722
Chicago, IL 60641-3053 Admitted: Oct. 5, 2013
Camellmeadows@earthlink.net
David Caldwell, NC, PS

962322 **Neilitz, Frances Leslie Glowienka (Mrs. Thomas LeRoy)**
N3116 W. Silver Lake Dr. H: (715) 942-2363
Waupaca, WI 54981-9551 Admitted: Oct. 5, 2016
tneilitz@charter.net
Samuel Hayes, NH, Capt PS; Lemuel Bishop, VT, Sgt

935178   **Parkhurst, Gena Marie**
P.O. Box 1914   H: (605) 716-5147
Rapid City, SD 57709-1914   Admitted: Aug. 5, 2014
gmp66@hotmail.com
William Brockett, SC, Capt

970599   **Pease, Elizabeth Sue Yeary (Mrs. William Morris)**
1124 Stirling Dr.   H: (859) 236-2175
Danville, KY 40422-2710   Admitted: July 5, 2017
bluekat1@live.com
Pleasant Terrell, VA, PS

872082   **Perry, Bonnie Lou Vaughn (Mrs. Roger Bruce)**
3300 N. Lake Shore Dr. Apt. 13A   H: (773) 929-3486
Chicago, IL 60657-3980   Admitted: July 6, 2009
bvperry@rcn.com
Thomas Paine, Jr, VA, Pvt; Edward Camp, NC, Sol;
Robert Paine, VA, Pvt; Solomon Deming, MA, Lt;
Thomas Paine, Sr, VA, PS

921186   **Robbins, Cameron Kerns Lane**
1183 Shore Rd.   C: (773) 259-1519
Cape Elizabeth, ME 04107-2112   Admitted: June 24, 2013
Robb1630@gmail.com
Isaac Worthen, NH, Smn

958742   **Stivers, Pamela Sue Wortham (Mrs. Richard)**
13227 N. Mimosa Dr. Unit 119   H: (812) 455-6331
Fountain Hills, AZ 85268-3644   Admitted: July 5, 2016
prstivers@gmail.com
Kinchen Martin, VA, Ens ; Hezekiah Hough, NC, CS PS;
William Wortham, NC, PS

908973   **Swanner, Sarah Augusta Thompson**
          (Mrs. Nicholas Brandon Arnett)
4470 Windsor Oaks Cir.   H: (773) 750 2982
Marietta, GA 30066-2324   Admitted: Oct. 6, 2012
sarahswanner@gmail.com
George Slayton, GA, Sol; Edward Wills, VA, Pvt

848211 **Swick, Martha Hoffman (Mrs. William Francis, Jr.)**
601 E. Church St.   H: (815) 467-3007
Minooka, IL 60447-8782   Admitted: Dec. 9, 2006
marthaswick@hotmail.com
Michael Vreeland, NJ, Pvt

468562 **Thompson, Susan Peables**
1360 N. Lake Shore Dr. Apt. 410   H: (312) 321-0040
Chicago, IL 60610-8440   Admitted: Oct. 16 1959
Isaiah Cushman, Jr, MA, Pvt

896399 **Williams, Jennifer Rae Lohrengel (Mrs. Ryan Matthew)**
204 Cottontail Ln.   H: (512) 688-3515
Georgetown, TX 78626-7525   Admitted: Oct. 8, 2011
jenniferwilliams.chapter.nsdar@gmail.com
Matthew Newton, CT, CS PS

572053 **Woodcock, Marcia Marie Hudson (Mrs. George W)**
422 N Cherry St   H: (618) 263-3745
Mount Carmel, IL 62863-2131   Admitted: Oct. 13, 1972
mhwoodcock@frontier.com
Jacob Keagy, PA, Mil ; Tobias Bickel, PA, PS

IN MEMORY OF

Joan Neumann

Lena Joan Neumann, 81, passed away January 25, 2019 at home. Joan was born Lena Joan Fleming in Holts Summit, MO. Preceded in death by her parents Roy Maiden Fleming and Mildred (Knife) Fleming and her brother Jerry Fleming. Joan is survived by her devoted husband of 60 years, Robert J. Neumann. Loving mother of Robert R. (Cathleen Hetland) Neumann and Craig J. (Aura Murphy) Neumann. Beloved grandmother of Karen (Ryan Bacastow) Neumann, Katherine, Ian and Camryn Neumann; beloved sister in law of Carolyn Unruh Fleming Puckett, dear aunt of Michael A. (Julianne Brown) Fleming and great aunt of Katelyn and Aidan. A private cremation was held, and her ashes were scattered in one of her favorite places. In lieu of flowers, take someone you love to lunch. "We knew you were here, we heard you laughing."

CHAPTER INVESTMENT FUNDS

Permanent Memorial and Endowment Fund
Established May 8, 1919 with a contribution from Mrs. Gilpin Moore (Jennie Corbly Moore, NSDAR #52506, 1905), and augmented by additional gifts and bequests from members, was placed in irrevocable trust on July 26, 1927. The income is specified for use by Chicago Chapter for patriotic, historical, and educational purposes.

Student Scholarship Fund
Established October 1935 by Mrs. Frederick J. Dickson (Sarah Deneen Dickson, NSDAR#128038, 1917) in memory of her parents. A memorial gift in the name of Miss Florence Deneen (NSDAR #50650, 1905), sister of Mrs. Dickson, was added in 1962. Individual contributions from members have been added to the principal through the years.
The yearly income is used for a college tuition scholarship given to a Chicago High School student selected by the Chapter for a Good Citizen award. A gift from the estate of Nancy Ellen Postma (NSDAR #579827, 1973) received in 1989 is designated for scholarship purposes.

Chapter Life Membership Fund
Established May 16, 1978 by the Chicago Chapter Regent, Mrs. David L. Ostfeld (NSDAR #501405, 1954), with fees paid by members Chicago Chapter Life Memberships.

Edith R. Friend Memorial Fund
Established 1956. Miss Edith R. Friend (NSDAR #327675, 1941). Robert S. Friend, brother of Edith R. Friend, added additional funds to the Edith R. Friend Fund in 1999 as a tribute to his sister's memory. In 2013, additional funds were donated to the memorial on behalf of Robert and Ilse Friend, this gift represents the final distribution.

Jessie Day Reilly Memorial Fund
Established 1980. Jessie Day Reilly (Mrs. J. Edward, NSDAR#348376, 1944).

Lillian A. Seinwerth Memorial Fund
Established 1982. Lillian Bourg Horn Seinwerth (Mrs. William J., NSDAR #281522, 1933).

Olive Falls Memorial Fund
Established 1983. Dr. Olive Falls (NSDAR#185431, 1923).

Koehler-Donaldson-Varney Memorial Fund
Established 1989 with a generous bequest from the Trust held in the name of Henry O. Koehler. Mr. Koehler, husband of Lois Howell Varney Donaldson Koehler (NSDAR #302067, 1937), died in 1984. Mrs. Koehler, her mother (Helen Varney Donaldson, NSDAR #38983, 1902), and her grandmother (Caroline Cadwallader Howell Varney, NSDAR #38932, 1902), were members of Chicago Chapter and life members of NSDAR.

Marguerite Bourg Ferris Memorial Fund
Established 1990. Marguerite Bourg Ferris
(Mrs. Carleton Gillespie, NSDAR #281507, 1933).

Lynette Sherman Memorial Fund
Established 2013. Frances Lynette Sherman (#455129, 1957).

BYLAWS OF THE CHICAGO Chapter of
THE NATIONAL SOCIETY OF THE
DAUGHTERS OF THE AMERICAN REVOLUTION
Revised February 18, 2017

ARTICLE I
Name.

The name of this Chapter shall be the Chicago Chapter of the National Society of the Daughters of the American Revolution.

ARTICLE II
Objects.

The objects of this Chapter shall be:

(1) to promote the objects of the National Society of the Daughters of the American Revolution, hereinafter referred to as the National Society or NSDAR;

(2) To perpetuate the memory and spirit of the men and women who achieved American independence, by the acquisition and protection of historical spots and the erection of monuments; by the encouragement of historical research in relation to the Revolution and the publication of its results; by the preservation of documents and relics, and of the records of the individual services of Revolutionary soldiers and patriots; and by the promotion of celebrations of all patriotic anniversaries;

(3) To carry out the injunction of Washington in his farewell address to the American people, "to promote, as an object of primary importance, institutions for the general diffusion of knowledge," thus developing an enlightened public opinion, and affording to young and old such advantages as shall develop in them the largest capacity for performing the duties of American citizens;

(4) To cherish, maintain and extend the institutions of American freedom; to foster true patriotism and love of country, and to aid in securing for mankind all the blessings of liberty.

ARTICLE III
Members.

Section 1. Eligibility.
Any woman is eligible for membership in the National Society of the Daughters of the American Revolution who is not less than eighteen years of age, and who is lineally descended from a man or woman who, with unfailing loyalty to the cause of American Independence, served as a sailor, or a soldier or civil officer in one of the several Colonies or States, or in the United Colonies or States or as a recognized patriot, or rendered material aid thereto, provided an applicant for Chapter membership is personally acceptable to the Chapter.

Section 2. Admission.
An applicant for membership through this Chapter shall be endorsed by two members of the Chapter who are in good standing and to whom the applicant is personally known. The Chapter may not discriminate against the applicant on the basis of race or creed. The acceptability of the applicant for Chapter membership shall be by a majority vote by ballot of the Chapter at a regular meeting. Within one year, unless granted an extension by the Chapter, the applicant shall submit to the Chapter all required documents, prepared in accordance with instructions established and distributed by the National Society, and accompanied by the prescribed fees and dues.
[NSDAR Bylaws Article III. Section 2 (a)]

Section 3. Transfers and Reinstatements.
A member desiring to join the Chapter by reinstatement, transfer from another chapter or from member-at-large shall be proposed and accepted by the Chapter by a majority vote by ballot in the same manner as a new member.

Section 4. Resignations.
A member desiring to resign shall present her resignation in writing to the Chapter Registrar, who shall immediately report the resignation to the Office of the Organizing Secretary General. A member whose dues are delinquent shall not be entitled to resign from membership.
[NSDAR Bylaws Article IV. Section 2 (e) (4).]

Section 5. Associates.
a.   The Chapter may, by a majority vote by ballot accept as associate member a member of another Chapter providing that any member so accepted shall be a Chapter member in good standing and may be an associate member in not more than two Chapters in a state at the same time.

b.   An associate member shall not be counted toward representation or have a right to vote or to hold an elected office in the Chapter.

ARTICLE IV
Fees and Dues.

Section 1. The application fee to the National Society shall be as determined by the Continental Congress.
[NSDAR Bylaws Article IV. Section 1. (a)]

Section 2. Annual Dues.
a.   The annual Chapter dues shall be twenty-five dollars ($25.00) plus the amount required by the National Society and the Illinois State Organization payable in advance on or before the 15th day of September of each year. A late fee of $10.00 will be assessed for all dues paid after October 1st.

b.   Dues for a member admitted or reinstated on or after July 5th by the National Board of Management shall be credited for the upcoming dues year which begins December 1.
[NSDAR Bylaws, Article IV, Section (c)]

c.   The dues and fees for readmission of a resigned member or a member dropped for non-payment of dues shall be as prescribed by the Bylaws of the National Society.
[NSDAR Bylaws Article IV, Section 4.]

d.   The annual dues of an associate member shall be ten dollars ($10.00) payable in advance on or before the 15th day of September of each year with the evidence of her membership in good standing in another Chapter. She shall pay no national or state dues through this Chapter.

e.   The annual national dues for each member shall be sent by the

Chapter Treasurer to the Office of the Organizing Secretary General, payable to the Treasurer General by the date and method established in the bylaws of the National Society. [NSDAR National, Article IV. Section 2 (a)]

f.   On October 1, the Chapter Treasurer shall notify all members whose dues have not been paid that their dues are delinquent and that such member is ineligible to vote in Chapter business. The National Society will terminate membership if dues are not received by the date and method established in the bylaws of the National Society. [NSDAR Bylaws, Article IV. Section 2(a)].

ARTICLE V
Officers.

Section 1. Officers.
a.   The elected officers of the Chapter shall be a Regent, First Vice Regent, Second Vice Regent, Chaplain, Recording Secretary, Corresponding Secretary, Treasurer, Registrar, Historian, Librarian.

b.   The offices of Chapter regent, Chapter recording secretary and Chapter treasurer shall be held by three separate Chapter member. [NSDAR Bylaws, Article XIII. Section 6 (a).]

Section 2. Eligibility.
a.   To be eligible for the office of Regent, a member shall have held membership in the Chicago Chapter for at least one continuous year preceding her election to office. In addition, a candidate for Regent shall have also served for at least two years on the Chicago Chapter Board of Management.

b.   To be eligible for the office of First Vice Regent or Second Vice Regent, a member shall: (i) be a member of the Chicago Chapter for one continuous year immediately preceding her election and (ii) have served for at least one year on the Chicago Chapter Board of Management.

c.   To be eligible for any other office, a member shall have belonged to the Chapter for one continuous year preceding her election to office. An exception to this can be made with the

permission of the National Board of Management.
[NSDAR Bylaws, Article XIII. Section 6(b)]

   d. No two members of the same family shall serve on the Board of Management at the same time.

ARTICLE VI
Board of Management Nomination, Election and Terms

Section 1. Nomination.

   a. In the year preceding an election a nominating committee consisting of five members shall be elected by the Chapter at the regular November Chapter meeting.

   b. In the event there is no regularly scheduled meeting in November, or a quorum is not present, the Regent may delay the vote until the January Business meeting or the Chicago Chapter Board of Management may call a special meeting with thirty (30) days notice to the Chapter.

   c. At its first meeting, the nominating committee shall elect its chairman from amongst its members. Three shall constitute a quorum. A member may not serve on the nominating committee more than once in two years. It shall be the duty of the nominating committee to nominate one candidate, whose consent to serve has been obtained, for each office to be filled.

Section 2. Election.

   a. The nominating committee shall first present the proposed slate at the regular February Chapter meeting. The nominating committee shall again present the proposed slate of officers at the regular March Chapter Meeting.

   b. Immediately following the March announcement by the nominating committee of the proposed slate additional nominations may be made from the floor, provided the consent of the nominee shall first have been obtained. Election of nominees shall then be held. If there is only one nominee for any, the election for that office may be made by voice vote. Otherwise, election for that office must be by ballot. A majority vote shall elect. There shall be no proxy voting.

Section 3.   Terms of Office.

a.   Officers shall be elected for a term of two years or until their successors are elected.

b.   The Regent, the First Vice Regent, the Recording Secretary, the Registrar and the Historian shall be elected in odd calendar years.

c.   The Second Vice Regent, the Chaplain, the Corresponding Secretary, the Treasurer and the Librarian shall be elected in even calendar years.

d.   The term of office shall begin at the close of the Continental Congress.

e.   Installation of officers can take place in May. No member shall serve more than two consecutive terms in the same office.

f.   A member who has served more than half a term in any office shall be considered to have served a term.

g.   Any outgoing Regent may not serve on the Board of Management for a period of two years thereafter.

Section 4 Vacancies.

a.   In case of a vacancy in the office of Regent, the First Vice Regent shall become Regent. In case of a vacancy in the office of First Vice Regent, the Second Vice Regent shall become First Vice Regent. In the event the First Vice Regent or Second Vice Regent is unwilling or not eligible to fill the vacancy due to requirements defined in Article V Section 2a or due to term limits as specified in Article V Section 3 above, the Board of Management shall fill the vacancy.

b.   The Board of Management will fill all other vacancies by appointment. The Chapter shall affirm the appointment for the unexpired term at a regular meeting.

Section 5. Compensation.

Board members receive no compensation except approved reimbursable expenses.

ARTICLE VII.
Duties of Officers.

Section 1. Duties.

The officers of the Chicago Chapter shall perform the duties prescribed by these bylaws, by the Bylaws of the National Society, the bylaws of the Illinois State Organization, by the parliamentary authority and such other duties as shall be ordered by the Chapter.

Section 2. The Regent shall:

a. preside at all meetings of the Chapter and of the Board of Management, and shall have general supervision of the affairs of the Chapter;

b. be the chief executive officer of the Chapter;

c. appoint all committee chairmen except the nominating committee;

d. appoint a Parliamentarian;

e. be ex-officio a member of all committees except the nominating committee; and

f. complete the Chapter Master Report, or ensure it is completed, and submit it as instructed.

Section 3. The First Vice Regent shall:

a. perform the duties and responsibilities of the Regent in her absence or inability to serve;

b. perform such other duties as the Board or Chapter requires including meeting location arrangements and refreshment facilitation; and

c. Keep a roll of current members.

Section 4. The Second Vice Regent shall:
a. perform the duties and responsibilities of the Regent in her and the First Vice Regent's absence or inability to serve; and

b. perform such other duties as the Board or Chapter requires, including Programs and Speaker introduction.

Section 5. The Chaplain shall:
a. conduct such religious services as required;

b. communicate, whenever possible, with members who are ill or in distress; plan memorial services for deceased members; and

c. notifies the State Chaplain of all deceased members.

Section 6. The Recording Secretary shall:
a. record the proceedings of the meetings of the Chapter and Board of Management;

b. be custodian of all records not otherwise provided for elsewhere; and

c. keep a role of members of committees.

Section 7. The Corresponding Secretary shall:
a. send notices of meetings;

b. conduct correspondence, newsletter, yearbook and communications as requested by the regent or required by action of the Chapter of the board of management.

Section 8. The Treasurer shall:
a. receive all funds of the Chapter and deposit them in a financial institution (or financial institutions) as may be designated by the Chapter or the Board of Management;

b. disburse funds as directed by the Chapter or Board of Management, and pay only those bills authorized by the Regent;

c. remit national dues to the Office of the Organizing Secretary General, and State dues to the State Treasurer prior to the first day of December, for every active member

d.   prepare the accounts for review before each Annual Meeting;

e.   provide financial reports to the Audit Committee or to an independent external auditor at the end of her term; and at the end of the Chapter's fiscal year

f.   have available at, or distribute before, the Annual Business Meeting a copy of the Chapter's financial statements including a statement of all income and expenditures for the operating accounts and funds of managed by the Chapter and

g.   submit the appropriate 990 form to the IRS on the fifteenth day of the fifth month following the end of the Chapter's fiscal year and provide verification of filing to the state treasurer

Section 9. The Registrar shall:
a.   furnish or make available an application to candidates whose acceptability has been favorably acted upon by the Chapter;

b.   ascertain, prior to submitting, that the application is in proper form and accompanied by properly prepared supporting documentation.

c.   confirm that together with the application and documentation, the proper fees are remitted as established by the current procedure of the National Society

d.   notify the Regent, Recording Secretary, Corresponding Secretary, Treasurer and new member of acceptance to membership

e.   notify the Registrar of the State organization, as required.

f.   upon transfer out of the Chapter, send the members's application to the member (if transfer is to member-at-large) or to the receiving Chapter in accordance with instruction of the National Society and

g.   report to the Office of the Organizing Secretary General, all changes in membership, marriage, divorce, deaths, resignations, transfers and changes of address as they occur

Section 10. The Historian shall:
a. direct such historical work as may be requested by the Chapter in accordance with the historical programs of the National Society and of the Illinois State Organization; and

b. be custodian of historical and biographical papers which the Chapter has or may acquire including maintaining inventory of Chapter archives and non-financial assets.

Section 11. The Librarian shall:
a. cooperate with the State Librarian in securing books for the DAR Library in Washington, DC and the Illinois DAR Library located in the C.E. Brehm Library in Mt. Vernon, Illinois;

b. and provide other library work as the National Society and the Illinois State Organization may authorize.

ARTICLE VIII
Meetings

Section 1. Monthly Meetings

The regular meetings of the Chapter shall be held on the third Saturday of each month from September to November, January to June inclusive, unless otherwise ordered by the Chapter or Board of Management. The regular meeting in February shall include George Washington's Birthday celebration and the first presentation of the Nominating Committees proposed slate of officers. The March meeting shall include the election of the new slate of officers. The regular meeting in May shall be the annual spring luncheon and shall end with the installation of the Chapter's new officers in attendance.

Section 2. Annual Meeting.

The regular meeting in January shall be known as the Annual Business Meeting and shall be for the purpose of receiving reports of officers and committees, and for any other business that may arise. The Annual Business Meeting shall be members only, if so designated by the Board of Management.

Section 3. Special Meetings.

Special meetings may be called by the Regent or by the Board of

Management or shall be called upon the written request of fifteen (15) members. Except in cases of emergency, the meeting will be arranged within five (5) days and five (5) days notice shall be given. The business transacted at any special meeting shall be limited to that stated in the call to the meeting. Special meetings shall be for Chapter members only.

Section 4. Electronic Meetings.

The majority of regular Chapter meetings shall be held in-person, except that provision may be allowed for members who are unable to attend in person to participate by electronic means, so long as all members can simultaneously hear each other and participate, subject to any limitations established in special rules of order adopted to govern such participation, and no expense to the Chapter. Electronic mail (e-mail) shall not be used to conduct meetings.

Section 5. Quorum and Proxy Voting

Fifteen (15) members of the Chapter shall constitute a quorum. There shall be no proxy voting.

Section 6. Notice

Unless members indicate otherwise to the Regent (and Corresponding Secretary or Recording Secretary) in writing, all communications required in these bylaws, including meeting notices may be sent using electronic mail.

Section 7. Cancelled Meetings.

In case of emergency, a simple majority of Chapter officers may collectively agree to cancel a regularly scheduled meeting due to adverse weather or other circumstances beyond the control of the Chapter or members. Every attempt will be made to provide timely notification to members.

ARTICLE IX
Board of Management.

Section 1. Officers.

The officers of the Chapter shall constitute the Board of Management. All members of the Board of Management shall be considered directors for purposes of Illinois state law to comply with the Articles of Incorporation.

Section 2. Authority.

The Board of Management shall have general supervision of the affairs of the Chapter between its meetings and shall make recommendations to the Chapter. The Board is subject to the orders of the Chapter and none of its acts shall conflict with action taken by the Chapter.

Section 3. Meetings.

Meetings of the Board of Management shall be held at the call of the Regent, or upon written request of four (4) of the executive board. Members who are not present in person may be permitted to participate by electronic means, so long as all members can simultaneously hear each other and participate, subject to any limitations established in special rules of order adopted by the executive board to govern such participation at no expense to the Chapter.

Section 4. Quorum.

A majority of the members of the Board of Management shall constitute a quorum.

Section 5. Non-members.

With the consent of the members of the Board of Management, the Regent may invite Chapter committee chairs to attend meetings of the Board of Management and to participate in discussion. Chapter committee chairs shall not make motions, second motions, or vote.

Section 6. Finances.

a.   All expenses or disbursements outside of the normal budget process or those not previously approved by the Board or the Chapter in excess of one hundred dollars ($100.00) shall be approved by the Board.

b.   All investment income and donations shall be used in support of the objects as described in Article II at the direction of the Chapter or the Board, unless the donor stipulates otherwise. Further all changes in the investments must be made at the explicit direction of the Board of Management.

Section 7. Board of Management Electronic Voting.

Electronic voting shall be permitted between board meetings only for important time sensitive issues that require a timely and more immediate decision. These motions must have a maker and second and provide sufficient time for e-mail discussion with a date for a final e-mail vote.

ARTICLE X
Committees

Section 1. General
a. Committee chairs shall be appointed by the Regent as the Chapter may authorize or as the National Society or the Illinois State Organization may require. Committees shall have a Chair whose term shall be two years or until a successor is appointed, her term to begin at the close of Continental Congress.

b. The National Committees are defined by the National Organization and their work is described on the Committee pages of the National members' website.

c. The State Committees are defined by the Illinois State Organization and are listed on the committee pages of the Illinois State Organization's members' website.

Section 2. Chapter Standing Committees.
a. The Audit Committee shall conduct a year-end review of the Chapter's financial books and records. No person shall serve on this committee who would concurrently be serving as Treasurer or serving on the Ways and Means Committee.

b. The Ways and Means Committee shall:
   (i) develop a proposed annual budget to be presented to the Board with the input of committee chairs and the Board;

   (ii) review the investments annually and provide recommendations to the Board and Chapter for investment maintenance or changes; and

   (iii) review recommendations for expenses outside of the budget cycle and provide recommendations to the Board. The Treasurer shall be a member of this committee, but not the chairman of this committee.

Section 3. Other.

a.   Such other committees, standing or special, shall be appointed by the Regent as the Chapter may authorize or as the National Society or the Illinois State Organization may require.

b.   The Meeting Committee shall assist the member of the Board of Management who handles programming with meeting coordination and shall assist with the set-up and clean-up of meeting facilities.

Article XI
Insurance and Chapter Assets

Section 1.

Any member or officer who has property of the Chapter must execute a proper agreement with the Chapter, which shall be filed with the Recording Secretary.

Section 2.

The Regent's pin shall be insured by the Chapter.

Section 3.

The Chapter's non-financial assets as maintained in a storage unit by the Chapter must be insured by the Chapter.

ARTICLE XII
Representation.

Section 1. Continental Congress.

The representation of the Chapter at Continental Congress shall be as provided in the Bylaws of the National Society.

Section 2. State Conference.

The representation of the Chapter at meetings of the Illinois State Organization shall be as provided in the bylaws of the Illinois State Organization.

Section 3. Delegates.

The Chapter shall elect delegates and alternates for Continental Congress at the meeting preceding the deadline for Continental Congress delegate notification. A member shall have belonged to the

Chapter at least one continuous year immediately preceding Continental Congress to be eligible to represent the Chapter, provided that a member admitted at the either of the National Board of Management meetings held immediately before and after the preceding Continental Congress shall be considered eligible to represent the Chapter.

Section 4.
The Chapter shall elect delegates and alternates for the Illinois State Conference at the meeting preceding the deadline for the Illinois State Conference delegate notification. A member shall have belonged to the Chapter at least one continuous year immediately preceding the Illinois State Conference to be eligible to represent the Chapter.

ARTICLE XIII
Parliamentary Authority

The rules contained in the current edition of Robert's Rules of Order Newly Revised shall govern the Chapter in all cases to which they are not inconsistent with the bylaws or any rulings of the National Society of the Daughters of the American Revolution, or any special rules of order of the Illinois State Organization, or of this Chapter.

ARTICLE XV
Amendment to Bylaws

Section 1.
The Bylaws Committee consisting of five (5) members at the first meeting shall elect its chairman from amongst its members. Three (3) shall constitute a quorum. Shall receive, investigate, consider and report on proposals for amendments to the bylaws.

Section 2.
These bylaws may be amended at any regular meeting of the Chapter by a two-thirds (2/3) vote, provided the proposed amendment has been submitted in writing at the previous meeting and all members have been notified at least thirty (30) days prior to the meeting where the vote is to be taken. Unless otherwise provided prior to its adoption or in the motion to adopt, an amendment shall take effect immediately upon its adoption.

Section 3.
Any amendment adopted by the National Society, or by the

Illinois State Organization affecting the work of this Chapter shall become the law of the Chapter without further notice. [NSDAR Bylaws, Article XV. Section 10. and Article XXI]

ARTICLE XV
Dissolution

Although the period of duration of the Chapter is perpetual, if for any reason the Chapter is to be dissolved or otherwise terminated, no part of the property of the Chapter or any of the proceeds shall be distributed to or inure to the benefit of any of the officers or members of the Chapter. Upon the dissolution of the Chapter, assets shall be distributed by the Board of Management to and only to the state organization as designated by the Chapter.

National Society Daughters of the American Revolution Chicago Chapter Conflict of Interest Policy

Members of the Chicago Chapter Board of Management (BOM) and Chapter Committee Chairs sign yearly conflict of interest statements. Board of Management and Committee Chair member understand that NSDAR is a charitable organization, and in order to maintain its federal tax exemption, it must engage primarily in activities which accomplish one or more of its tax-exempt purposes. Board of Management members agree that they have not received direct or indirect compensation in any amount or gifts or favors in excess of $100 value from any entity or person that has/had or is negotiating a transaction or arrangement with Chicago Chapter of NSDAR.

If there are any items or compensation they must list such items and their approximate value. These agreements are on file with the Chicago Chapter Recording Secretary.

National Society Daughters of the American Revolution Property Agreement

Chicago Chapter Board of Management Members sign Property Acceptance and Agreements acknowledging that they have a fiduciary responsibility to protect and safeguard the property of the Chicago Chapter that they have and do declare that in their capacity.
They provide the location and description of any chapter property and instruction for their heirs, trustees, successors, assigns, and personal representatives that in the event of their incapacity, illness, or death, they shall immediately contact and advise the Chapter Regent or Secretary to retrieve the above listed property and return it to the Chapter.
This Agreement shall also be construed and enforced in accordance with the law of the jurisdiction in which the Chapter listed above holds its charter.

National Society Daughters of the American Revolution Member Photo Consent Agreement

Members authorize the Chicago Chapter of the National Society Daughters of the American Revolution (NSDAR), to use, reproduce, and/or publish photographs and/or video that may pertain to me including image, likeness and/or voice without compensation. Members understand that this material may possibly be used in various publications, public affairs releases, recruitment materials, broadcast public service announcements (PSAs) or for other related endeavors. This material may also appear on the NSDAR's Internet Web Page.

This authorization is continuous and may only be withdrawn by a member's specific rescission of this authorization. Consequently, the NSDAR or chapter affiliates may publish materials, use the name, photograph, and reference me as deemed appropriate in order to promote/publicize the NSDAR goals of historic preservation, education and patriotism.

Articles and Artifacts from the Archives

A history of the Chicago Chapter NSDAR is also a history of the founding of the National Society and the Illinois State Organization with the presence of many of the same women.

Chicago Chapter Member, Margaret Forney Becker, has published a collection of the most important articles from the Chapter's scrapbooks including newspaper articles, photographs and programs. Every Chapter member will want to have a copy of this special Chapter history.

Articles and Artifacts was published in honor of the Chicago Chapter's 125th anniversary. Copies of the book are $40. Please email thefirstchapterdarchicago.org for information on how to get your copy. It makes a great gift.

Notes:

Made in the USA
Monee, IL
26 August 2019